MAKING IT IN COUNTRY MUSIC

OTHER BOOKS BY SCOTT FARAGHER

Music City Babylon
The Branson, Missouri, Scrapbook
The Complete Guide to Riverboat Gambling

★ ★ ★

MAKING IT IN COUNTRY MUSIC

An Insider's Guide to Launching or Advancing Your Career

SCOTT FARAGHER

A Citadel Press Book
Published by Carol Publishing Group

A Citadel Press Book
Published by Carol Publishing Group
Citadel Press is a registered trademark of Carol Communications, Inc.

For editorial, sales and distribution, and queries regarding rights and
permissions, write to Carol Publishing Group, 120 Enterprise Avenue,
Secaucus, N.J. 07094

In Canada: Canadian Manda Group, One Atlantic Avenue, Suite 105,
Toronto, Ontario M6K 3E7

Carol Publishing Group books are available at special discounts
for bulk purchases, sales promotions, fund-raising, or educational
purposes. Special editions can also be created to specifications.

Manufactured in the United States of America
10 9 8 7 6 5 4 3 2 1

Library of Congress Cataloging-in-Publication Data

Faragher, Scott.
    Making it in country music : an insider's guide to launching
or advancing your career / Scott Faragher.
        p.   cm.
    "A Citadel Press book."
    Includes index.
    ISBN 0-8065-1710-7 (pbk.)
    1. Country music—Vocational guidance. I. Title.
ML3790.F36   1995
781.642'023'73—dc20   95-19251
                                            CIP
                                            MN

Doug Parker, M.D. 1949-1995

This book is dedicated to Doug Parker, M.D. of Fort Smith, Arkansas, who believed in, encouraged, and supported my writing, long before I was even close to being published. He supported many musicians financially and otherwise during his life, from country, to Jamaican reggae, to English rock. Those who knew him closely benefited greatly from his friendship, generosity, and sense of humor and irony. He shall be greatly missed.

We both endured a great deal, went through many ups and downs, made mistakes and learned from most of them. We shared our dreams and had fun. Thanks, Doug.

Also, to everybody who has the courage to follow their dreams.

CONTENTS

ACKNOWLEDGMENTS

Due to the nature of my first book, *Music City Babylon*, there were many persons I spoke with in preparing this book who, while very helpful, preferred that their names not be mentioned. All of you know who you are, and your help is most appreciated.

Many thanks to the others who have helped me in the preparation of this book, either by their observations and their patient answers to questions, or by their actions, positive or negative. Norbert Nix of Mercury Records, for his valuable help on the sections dealing with record promotion and artist development; Terry Worthington at United Way; Gavin promoter Jerry Duncan; Paul Loveless at CDX; Lisa Austin at Gavin; programming consultant Rick Shane; promoter Susan Turner with Schindler-Turner Promotions; Miles Bell at Williams-Bell; Wade Jessen at *Billboard*; Lon Helton at *Radio and Records*; tour manager and master of personal security Steve Wallach; managers Don Light and Jack McFadden; attorney Ralph Gordon; Roger Sovine, Harry Warner, Ima Withers, and Keith Mohsinger at BMI; producer and publisher Tom Collins; Kent Glaser, BMI; songwriters Larry Weiss, Paul Craft, and Ed Mugavero; Amy Kurland and the Bluebird Cafe; Peter Lippman at Lippsync; Steve Brallier, for reminding me why I started writing; Chad Selden, in Memphis, Chuck Glaser, for giving me my first job in the music business twenty-two years ago; to great fellow writers Steve Eng and Steve Womack.

Thanks also to David and Sandy Brokaw at the Brokaw Company, always the best in PR and artist management.

Thanks also to my son, Scott, for his understanding of the loss of time. Thanks to Hillel Black for supporting my ideas, and believing in and encouraging my writing endeavors.

Aboogala! Traditional African greetings to Dick Kwame Lewis at Cafe Apa Dapa, Mozambique.

Thanks also to all of the local greats who make Nashville such a wonderful place; Naresh at Sitar, the best damned Indian joint west of Chattanooga; The Great Escape, Nashville's best used-record store and research center; Hillwood Wrecker Service; Satsuma, Nashville's best place for lunch; The Corner Market; Shelton Gallery, Nashville; Richard Jett and all of my bankers at Bud's Liquors; Robert and Bobby Ryan; the Country Music Association; attorney John Lentz; attorney John Mason; Mark Shenkel and all the folks at Gibson Guitars; Tower Books and Records; Davis-Kidd Booksellers; and Bookstar. Thanks also to David Spear; Robb Corless; Alan Butler; the Seldens in Tunica, Mississippi; Eddie Rhines; Joann Berry, World Class Talent; Bruce Honick, *Country Weekly*.

Thanks also to the folks at Ingram Distributors. Sincere appreciation to Dr. Constantine Chambers, one of Nashville's most famous and best-kept secrets.

Thanks also to Belmont and Middle Tennessee State Universities for their excellent and ever-expanding music and music business programs.

Thanks again to Mark Page, and all of the personal fitness trainers at the Club, Bellevue and Green Hills.

Last but not least, thanks to Katherine Harrington for her constant support, advice, and companionship.

INTRODUCTION

Before we examine the subjects which follow, it might be a good idea to define the term "making it." The expression has a different meaning for each person entering the music business, whether as artist, writer, or business executive.

For some, the only possible definition of success is to be signed to a multimillion-dollar record or publishing deal and to be an international superstar. For others, it may mean being the president of a major record label, writing multi-platinum-selling songs, or becoming a successful artist manager.

Those in search of fame and fortune in Nashville share similar dreams. For some, they become a reality. For others, dreams can become a liability, in that smaller but significant advances in a career tend to be undervalued in light of larger goals. Success in the music business in Nashville is a realistic goal which is attainable by most, in one form or another. The person who has decided to move to Nashville and become a singer, writer, musician, publisher, or music business executive can be successful and can make a living at his or her chosen profession without necessarily living at the very top of the field. For example, there are many recording acts, and singers, even some without record deals, who play listening rooms, clubs, and other engagements all over the country. They earn a very good living, in addition to having achieved the personal satisfaction of doing what they set out to do.

Success as an artist exists on many levels, and the

aspiring artist who moves to Nashville for a while to pursue his craft might end up as a successful act nationally, regionally, or even locally. Furthermore, anyone who is doing what he wants to do with his life, and is being paid to do it, is successful.

If making music is your objective, Nashville is the place to be and there are many opportunities to do that. Nashville is a boom town, and enough good jobs exist to allow the musician or artist to play at night without having to wash dishes or clean sewers during the day.

The present status of the American job market is another consideration. Seemingly every day we are bombarded by news of some misspent pension, or of medical benefits being taken away from some retired worker who had dutifully worked at the same job for thirty years. This being the case, the job security which many of our parents or grandparents took for granted no longer exists for most of us. Companies are bought up, taken over, or dissolved, and the worker who thought that he would have a job for life suddenly finds himself on the street. Security under present conditions is no longer something which can safely be trusted to others or found outside oneself.

If you have a good job and are happy with your present circumstances, then there is much to be said for your situation. You may do well and get by just fine, but chances are that you will never be rich, no matter how hard you work, or how good you happen to be at what you do. At least by pursuing your dream, the chance exists that you will be rich if you are successful in the artistic field. Getting rich is unlikely at most everyday jobs. The time has never been better to break away from the crowd and risk doing what you want to do with your life.

Ultimately, music is a calling, and if that is your approach, rather than "I think I can do it for a while and get rich," then you are already on the right track. If you have been given the gift of musical ability, and it brings you satisfaction to express yourself in that way, then chances are good that you will succeed. It is rare that the really talented leave Nashville in defeat.

If, on the other hand, you need to make a certain amount of money by such and such a date, you might be better off doing something else. Make certain that your motivations are right. If you feel that you are talented, and you enjoy excitment, making music, meeting new people, reaching new goals, and enjoying a sense of accomplishment, then you have picked the right field.

It should also be mentioned that there is no one way to make it in the music business. There are as many different roads to success as there are successful people. Ultimately, you will determine your own path, and your success or failure will rest on your own shoulders.

MAKING IT IN COUNTRY MUSIC

1

The Artist

The artist is the highest and most important part of the music business food chain. Everything and everybody within the music business exists to serve him, whether songs and songwriters, talent agents, record companies, managers, publicists, recording studios, musicians, recording equipment, musical instruments, studios, record companies, record promoters, music business attorneys, show promoters, ticket agencies, radio stations, or program directors. Indeed, every related aspect of the entire music business machine depends on the artist for its very existence.

To the degree that an artist is commercially successful, he is able to avail himself of the best elements of the above services with the greatest ease. But the relationship is seldom smooth for the artist, and he must constantly court the fickle favor of all of these entities if he is to survive and prosper.

Artists, singers, and entertainers generally fall into one of several categories at any given time in their careers. For this reason, I have arbitrarily decided to classify artists in the following manner. The categories will be found to apply across the board to artists in all categories of music.

The Artist on the Way Up

"On the way up" is a relative term, since few artists' careers are moving parallel. On the way up for one artist might mean being discovered by someone important at a record company. It might mean an artist's first television appearance, or it could mean the first time an artist fills a 10,000 seat arena as a headliner. On the way up, therefore, means different things to different artists.

On the way up can be the best time in an artist's life, both for himself and for those who work with him. For the moment at least, the artist on the way up has been smiled upon by fate.

Dealing with an artist at this stage of his career is usually fun. He's often in a good mood, is still appreciative of his team's efforts, and is willing to take direction. At this point he is still anxious to do interviews, pleasantly answers stupid questions, and feels happy that the press takes an interest in his work and his career. The artist looks forward to each new day as another opportunity to move ahead, closer to his goals.

At the same time, this can be tumultous for the artist and his associates, as the various players jockey for position and power. The artist will be pulled in many conflicting directions and forced into making important business and personal decisions which will influence the course of his future, positively or negatively. Often, and especially in the case of a younger artist, these decisions must be made before the artist really has garnered enough experience to correctly determine what's in his own best interests.

The Artist at the Top

For artists at the top, as for artists on the way up, there are several levels of success. The artist who consistently produces hit records and earns a good living doing shows often becomes a problem at this stage in his career. Some of the fear he felt, wondering whether he would make it or not, has started to diminish, and he is likely to feel like he can relax a bit. If this is the case, the artist might have fallen into the age-old trap of believing his own publicity. He sees himself in the paper, on TV, and in magazines, and he begins to think that he really is that great.

At this point, one of two paths are chosen by the artist, either intentionally or unconsciously. As difficult as it is to get to the top, it's much harder to stay there. Either the artist accepts that he has been blessed by God or destiny, and hopes to make the ride last as long as possible, or he becomes an egomaniac and begins the walk down the path which will eventually lead to the destruction of his career and most likely everything which went with it. With few exceptions, artists choose the latter course.

Every artist has an ego, and most artists need to be adored by the masses. Many artists need this constant input and approval. The artist who has made it to the upper level and turns into a jerk is headed for a fall. He will start to order around the people closest to him, if he hasn't done so already, often intentionally embarrassing them in front of their peers and associates. He may become verbally abusive to his spouse or girlfriend, or display negative behavior in a number of other ways, such as refusing to play certain types of shows, canceling dates without notice, and acting like a bigger jerk than usual around his agent, manager, and publicist.

The artist will use this newfound power. He remembers the agent who wouldn't meet with him, the manager who was too busy with other clients, the idiot at the record company who passed him by, the publisher who said he couldn't write, the good looking girl who wouldn't go out with him, the investor who didn't think he had a chance in hell of making it, the banker who wouldn't give him a loan—the list goes on and on. Now the tables are turned. When this happens, many artists want to make somebody, and sometimes everybody, pay for the hurt, rejection, and humiliation they suffered on the way up. This is, of course, self-destructive behavior. The artist whose behavior induces his agent, manager, band members, friends, and ultimately his fans to hate him will crash and burn sooner or later. Since there are other artists on the way up who are snapping at his heels, it usually doesn't take too long.

At this poiont, the wise artist will assume an air of humility and will go out of his way to meet and greet, and be the best he can be. It's harder to stay at the top than it is to get there. While this platitude sounds reasonable, it can only be understood fully by those who have made it to the top. The artist who has and who wants to stay will take a long look at how he got there and determine what he can do to stay there as long as possible.

The Artist on the Way Down Five, Four, Three, Two—Yo, Time Is Up.

The artist on the way down is possibly the worst of all. Usually, the artist doesn't realize that he's already dead.
He knows that something is wrong, but he doesn't know exactly what. His agency isn't getting him enough dates, so he fires the agency and moves to another. The record company can't seem to give his records the right kind of promotion, so he blames the people at the record label because they aren't doing their job. And so it goes, all the way down the line. Everybody is at fault for the situation—everybody, that is, except the artist.

He still has his ego, however, and continues to make demands and blame everyone in his circle. He was the genius who got his career started and maintained it to begin with.

He certainly hasn't lost any of his intellectual capacity. It must be those idiots who surround him. All the agency has to do is answer the phone and take orders. They can't even get that right. The manager is really being paid for doing nothing. The artist on the way down has already suffered a decline in revenue-producing capability, so those around him will turn their attentions to other artists, those on the way up.

The Artist Who Never Made It

There are several subcategories to this particular heading. The artist who never made it often ends up in some other branch of the music business. He may have had a record deal that didn't work, so he returned to songwriting or became a record producer, promoter, booking agent, or manager. Many successful people in all of these fields started out as artists. At some point, they realized that it wasn't going to happen for them as artists. They might have freaked out at first, but having eventually accepted the situation, they made the appropriate adjustments and successfully moved into a related branch of the music business.

Others returned to their hometowns with the satisfaction that they gave it their best effort. Those who tried and failed are not failures, provided they truly gave their absolute best. At the very least, they satisfied their curiosity and most likely learned priceless lessons about themselves and about life. The artist who halfway tried, but might have made it had he worked harder, will probably live a life of regret.

The Artist Who Never Will Make It

The artist who never will make it is a sad sight indeed. He may have a good buzz going with all types of industry heavyweights wanting to be involved in his career at the proper time. They come see his show, watch his performance, agree that he may very well be one of the greatest acts or singers they've ever seen or heard, and yet, for some reason, the act doesn't get signed. There are glowing articles in the paper, talks about record and publishing deals, but for some reason, nothing happens. This is a hard reality to face, and many artists refuse to face it at all, but time passes, and they get older, and still they keep on. Twenty years later, the artist ends up playing in some Mexican restaurant on weekends at happy hour with a guitar and a drum machine, still using the same picture he used years earlier, though it scarcely resembles him now.

What happened? There are many answers to the question. Each case is different. For some artists, it just doesn't happen. There's no real reason; success just never reaches beyond a certain level. Many artists stop the train themselves by doing stupid things, almost as if there were some hidden subconscious desire to fail. Others self-destruct long before they even get close to a career. As soon as things start moving, they suddenly decide that they are the geniuses, that everything which is happening in their careers is a result of their incredible brainpower, talent, and managerial skills. They foolishly cast aside the people who brought them to the point that there was a buzz to begin with. Many of them are just plain stupid.

There is a major difference between ignorance and stupidity. The ignorant artist can learn and in many cases desperately wants to learn, everything he can. The stupid artist figures he's already smarter than everyone in his immediate circle, so it would be best if he directs his own career and lets the manager follow his instructions. The statement is often made in legal circles that the man who represents himself has a fool for a client. The same usually goes for the artist who manages himself, regardless of his talent, because there is almost always the presence of one or more major character flaws which will guarantee that he won't make it.

And then there are those who not only will never make it but will never even get close. Perhaps they lack talent or looks or good communication skills. There are plenty of people who have the desire, make the commitment, and theoretically do everything necessary, but who for some reason never succeed. It happens often, and they return home after several weeks, months, or years. Maybe they thought the world would beat a path to their door. Whatever the reason or reasons, for these people, success never comes.

The Responsibilities of the Artist

Most management contracts specify that the artist agrees to pursue the development of his craft as an artist. Many persons with whom I spoke expressed the opinion that the artist should be available and on call twenty-four hours a day, seven days a week, year in and year out. This is a good idea. If an artist is working at a restaurant in order to get by, he is likely to be missing valuable opportunities to advance himself as a result of being unavailable.

On the other hand, most people at the upper end of the music business respect anyone who is working to support their desire for success, and will often make allowances in scheduling to accommodate someone. The fact that an aspiring artist is working because he has to, generally indicates that the artist is serious about his work, a fact which is usually looked upon favorably. Everybody has to start somewhere, and survival is the first rule of business.

What Goes Up Must Come Down

What about the artist who has worked hard for years playing bars, opening for major acts passing through town, who finally gets his big break? Let's run through a typical scenario. The particular details can vary considerably as to how the artist got started as a singer. Perhaps he developed a love for music as a child. Perhaps he was exposed to country radio from an early age, or maybe his father played guitar and sang for fun at local clubs after work, or his mother sang at church. By whatever means, an interest in music developed in the would-be artist, either at an early age or later, possibly in high school. The artist, in all probability, received an instrument, most likely a guitar, and learned or taught himself to play.

He encountered others with similar interests and started or joined a local band. The music they played was the same music they heard on the radio, cover tunes of the songs being played at the time, anything from rock to country. Eventually the band was good enough to play for money at local dances, shopping center openings, and so on.

Some members dropped out for one reason or another, or the band may have even dissolved altogether, but the singer has decided that this is what he wants to do with his life.

He has no idea how to go about it, but begins working on his career full-time, and starts writing his own songs as well. What's next?

Eventually the artist ends up in Nashville—Music City, U.S.A., home of the Grand Ole Uproar, the place where everything happens in country music. He may have moved .to Nashville without knowing anyone, or he may have developed a friendly relationship with an act he opened for earlier who had passed through his hometown.

The singer works hard, trying to find places to play in Nashville. He networks, sings at writer's nights, meets other artists and writers, but nothing is really happening, or so it seems. He runs out of money fairly quickly and takes a job as a waiter at night so that he can work during the day, writing with other artists and shopping his material around town.

Finally some publisher likes his material and lets him demo one song which he has written. The publisher wants to use the singer's voice to help him sell the song to a producer for a famous artist. The publisher gives the song to a producer friend in passing at lunch one day. The producer puts the tape on in his car, not that he really wants to hear it. He's been listening to bad music all day, but he promised the guy who gave it to him. He listens to the opening notes blankly and mindlessly as he stops at some fast-food joint to get a cup of coffee on the way back to his office. He doesn't even hear the first song as he places his order and digs around in the console of his car for some change.

He gets his coffee and pulls away from the drive-through window as the second song comes on. He isn't listening to the singer's voice. After all, this is some half-assed demo. He's listening to the melody and the lyrical content of the song.

The song is okay, nothing special. It's not bad, but it's not great either. But the singer—there is a certain raw quality to his voice, a certain edge. He's not bad. The producer rewinds the tape to the beginning of the first song. His car phone interrupts him and he takes the call, forgetting all about the singer and the two songs on the tape machine in his car.

Later that night, after a business meeting at dinner and four hours in a recording studio, the producer starts his drive home. Suddenly he remembers the tape in his car stereo and decides to give it a second listen. Yes, the kid has got something in his voice. Is the budding artist who sang the demos the same person who wrote the songs? The next day, he has to work on mixing some songs he cut the previous week. About noon he calls the publisher who gave him the tape and gets some information on the singer. No, the publisher doesn't have his address or phone number, but the young writer will most likely drop by in a couple of days. The publisher will have him call the producer when he shows up.

The producer takes the singer into a studio at his expense on a speculative basis. If he can get the singer a record deal, he will get some points or will produce the artist himself. Either way there is not necessarily any great commitment on the producer's part. He has too many irons in the fire already. He'll just call so-and-so over at the record company when the project is done, and get his reaction. If it works, great. If not, nothing lost.

In the meantime, the aspiring artist is so excited he can hardly live with himself. This is what he has wanted all of his life, why he came to town in the first place. He doesn't want to jinx his chances by thinking about it too much, but it really could happen for him. He could get that phone call from somebody big at the record company telling him that they want to sign him. After all, this is Nashville. The producer is a famous and important person in the Nashville music business. That he is willing to produce a trial session and hire real musicians at his own expense is incredible luck for the singer.

The singer goes into the studio to record with professional studio musicians, and gives it his best shot. Now it's up to the gods and the music business machine. While the singer continues to work at the restaurant, he waits for word from the producer. He wants to call him every five minutes to ask him if he's heard anything, but he knows that things move slowly in the music business. He doesn't want to seem any more an amateur than he is. It could be weeks before somebody at the record company even listens to the tape. In the meantime, he's sweating nails.

Then one night when the artist gets home from work, he finds a message on his answering machine. "This is so-and-so. They want to talk to you about a deal. Call me tomorrow. It sounds good." The artist and the producer meet with someone at the record label, and a deal is made. Contracts are drawn up and signed, and time passes. Material is selected, a recording schedule is set, a producer is determined, music is recorded, mixed, and mastered, and the artist's first project is ready. He goes to an expensive dinner and celebrates this important milestone in his life. He plays his copy of the tape for friends, family, fellow workers at the restaurant, and anyone else who will listen. He is justifiably proud of his hard work, his persistence, and his belief in himself.

Behind the scenes at the record label, a single is chosen and a release date is set. Announcements are made, a photo session takes place, a marketing plan is devised, and the artist performs a show for the record company personnel. An attorney and manager are chosen, an agency selected, an album released, band members auditioned, dates set, money borrowed, transportation arranged, and the artist's career is underway.

Irrespective of any other considerations, the bottom line is that an aspiring artist has ended up in Nashville, got a record deal, and is up at bat. The time, effort, and luck involved also vary for each artist, ranging from overcoming impossible odds after years of effort, to being at the right place at the right time and almost tripping over wonderful opportunities and circumstances. How the artist arrived and how long it took to get to the plate have little to do with the way things turn out for the majority of aspiring artists.

Most of them won't make it, no matter what they do or how good they are. There may be many reasons or no reasons. The record company changes bosses, and the man who signed the artist is dismissed; or several major artists release singles at the same time as the new artist, and the new one can't get airplay. Maybe someone at the record label doesn't like the artist or is pushing a different new artist, his own pet project.

Maybe the radio stations have been recently flooded with new singers and want to devote their airtime to proven hitmakers. Perhaps there are too many ballads on the air right now, or maybe too many fast songs, or too many love songs, or too many drinking songs.

The better the excuse, the worse it is, but for whatever reason or reasons, the artist's first single is unimpressively received by radio and by the public. The same with the second single release. Album sales are also extremely poor. A second album may be released, and it might show some promise, but it does nothing either. The former enthusiasm displayed by the artist's support team and by the people at the record label has diminished perceptibly as they've sensed that this project is a loser and, are directing their attention to new and hopefully more successful undertakings.

The artist is dropped from the record label, and his career, that for which he had worked so long, is for all practical purposes over. Whether he was dropped after one album or two, whether the process took eight months or two years, the result is the same. The career never really got started.

If you doubt this scenario, take a trip to a local used-record store and thumb through the country section. You will find dozens, if not more than a hundred former artists' albums. Some of the artists are well known but no longer have a record deal, even after years of radio success.

You'll find others, most of whom were on major record labels, whose names you vaguely remember or more likely won't recognize. You will be truly amazed that there have been that many artists signed by major record labels over the past twenty years who never made it or who only made it for a year or two.

This type of thing has been happening in popular music as long as it has been recorded, and probably even before that. It has also always happened in country music. As we've discussed elsewhere, the artist in country music today who has had a twenty-year career is a rarity.

How the artist handles himself at this juncture will determine whether he has a career from this point forward. If he was arrogant and acted as if the world owed him a living, spoke badly of his peers, and backstabbed the people who helped him, it is likely that the favor will be returned in kind. If he thought that his manager was an idiot, and that the people at the record company didn't know what they were doing, and that he was smarter than everybody else, there is a high probability that this will be his final stop on the road to stardom. While the possibility really does exist that everybody is an imbecile but himself, it is unlikely. Even if it were true, the chances of convincing everyone else in power that he was smarter than they are is unlikely.

The bad news is that the artist no longer has a record deal. The good news is that while many fall through the cracks at this point and lose their careers forever, it is also true that almost every truly successful artist today has suffered similar setbacks in the past. If these unfortunate circumstances have befallen you, remember that it is possible to survive and prosper. You can and must move ahead. If somebody in a position of power thought you had enough potential to sign you in the first place, when so many hundreds of other artists never get signed at all, the chances are that you really do have something to offer and that your potential is real and not imagined. Your next moves are critical.

First of all, you need to find out what went wrong with your first set of circumstances. You must fearlessly assess every aspect of your own personality before you attempt any further forward movement. If there is some fault in your own makeup, personality, or actions, you need to find, examine, and correct it. You won't get by merely acknowledging the problem and passing over it. It must be removed with as little passion as a surgeon would remove a diseased organ.

This fearless and thorough self-examination is not something which you can conclude over a couple of beers and dinner with some friends. It will take time, and things are very likely to get worse before they get better. This period of time represents a significant point in your personal quest and in your development as an artist and as a person. If you have approached your career as if it were a war up to this point, it may be wise to reflect on the battles you have won and lost. Examine your strengths and weaknesses, and take corrective measures.

The Artist as a Product

Many artists mistakenly imagine that the people they work with automatically view them as musical artists, stars, and personalities, rather than as products who exist to be marketed. While most associates at a local level do view artists as individuals, like them, and enjoy the relationships, there are others, elsewhere, who know an artist by name only, and then only to the extent that the artist's name matches up with an identifying account number in a computer somewhere.

These people, who the artist doesn't even suspect exist, often have a great deal of power over the disposition of an artist's career. They are the accountants and hard-core businessmen who look only at figures. The profit-and-loss statement is the only record they care about. The artist and his music are merely the medium of financial exchange. The artist is a product, to the people who make, sell, promote, and market the records, to the club, concert, fair, or other promoter who is using the artist as a product to sell tickets, to the songwriters who provide the artist a medium of expression, to the managers, agents, and publishers who seek to make the artist a valuable product.

If I'm Truly Great, Why Do I Have to Struggle So Hard?

This is a legitimate question, and one which perplexes many aspiring artists. There is no one answer, but there are several responses which are at least partially valid. To begin with, let's look at dress. In the first place, it's all been done before. Country music has already seen every kind of stage attire available, from the magnificent and colorful early cowboy-influenced rhinestone suits of the forties, fifties, and sixties, to the jeans and casual look of the outlaws in the seventies, to the West Coast–influenced pop attire of the eighties, to the mixture of styles and stylelessness which is pervasive today.

In terms of the country artist's image, we've seen everything from the rough but tender cowboy who sings as well as fights, like Roy Rogers, to the tough-guy jailbirds like Johnny Cash, Merle Haggard, and David Alan Coe, to the romantic balladeer, like Roy Orbison, to the tuxedo-clad symphony singer, to the young beautiful female, to the older female, to the styles of Emmylou Harris to Dolly Parton, to the folk singer, to the vocal groups, from the Sons of the Pioneers to Sawyer Brown, and everything else in between. It's all been done before.

The same thing applies musically as well. Country music has already heard the melodic voice, the loud howlers, the soft, sensuous voices, the nasal bluegrass whiners, the harmonies of vocal groups, and a fair amount of novelty songs as well. We've heard strings, steel guitars, rock guitars, accoustic guitars, violins and fiddles, banjers (banjos) drums, pianos, organs, synthesizers, and every other instrument available. As far as anyone knows, it's all been done and usually by someone who is truly great.

Part of the question for the aspiring artist today is, what can he bring to the musical table that is new and different but will also be accepted by record companies, radio stations, and ultimately the public? Again, it is possible that within the industry, and also with the public, nobody really wants anything but the status quo. Does the public really want great music? Does it really matter anyway? And what about the radio stations? Do they really care about "excellence in broadcasting," or are they just out to sell advertising? These are tough questions, especially since there are often conflicting agendas among the different players in the music business field.

Ultimately, if the artist is to succeed, he must assess the entire world of country music, including his image, music, talents, and liabilities. And he must determine who he really is musically. This must then be clearly defined, honed, polished, and successfully marketed by the artist, manager, agency, publicist, and record company.

Jobs

The artist moving to Nashville is usually faced with the need or desire to get a job. For many artists, this may mean working at a restaurant or club at night and shopping their material to publishers, managers, and record companies during the day. For others, it may mean the opposite, working at a day job and playing at night. There are few opportunities for the newcomer to Nashville who has the expectation of finding work as a singer as soon as he hits town. In the first place, there are many clubs offering "writers' nights," where aspiring singers and songwriters wait in line to play free, just for the chance to have their mateiral heard. In other words, there is a great deal of competition for singing jobs. Before you can get a job, people must know who you are, that you are available, and what you can do. This can only be accomplished by taking the initiative yourself, making the rounds, networking, and getting known. There is always a place for anyone who deserves to be there, but it's up to you to hustle and find out where you belong.

Nashville is growing at an unprecedented rate, and new job possibilities are opening up daily. There are new music publishing companies, new nightclubs, new recording studios, new acts going on tour, and new businesses moving to town. There is a jobs section at the end of almost every chapter in this book, and suggestions have been given there for finding specific types of related work. There are jobs available for singers who are resourceful and willing to take the trouble to seek them out.

The *Nashville Banner* and the *Tennessean*, the two daily papers, the *Nashville Scene*, *Music Row*, and other papers and magazines which are readily available on racks, at bookstores, and cafes, provide up-to-date information on new club openings. The new incorporations

and companies sections of local papers list new businesses and their areas of endeavor. Several successful
national acts have started by working shows at Opryland.
If you have a good voice, it's possible to get a job as a demo
singer for publishing companies. There is nightclub work
and studio work as backup singer.

The possibilities are unlimited for the aspiring singer
who is willing to look beneath the surface to the "We don't
have anything available right now" response and keep
pushing. This book is devoted to explaining how things
work in Nashville, what to look for, what to expect, and
what to avoid. The information which follows will be
helpful to you in practice, to the degree which you are
willing to take the personal initiative to transform your
dreams into reality.

2

The Attorney

Don't Sign Anything Without Having an Attorney

This is one of the first and most important rules of the music business. The attorney is the first person with whom you should have any professional business dealings. So many artists, songwriters, and musicians get involved in bad management, publishing, or recording deals because they failed to have proper legal representation going into a deal. You will probably need an attorney at every significant point in your career. It's better to have one at the beginning, before there is a problem. As the old saying goes, prevention is better than a cure.

The Relationship With an Attorney

The music industry has become so complicated that the majority of artists in Nashville have no clue as to what any contract actually means. The average artist, despite his intelligence, is likely to find himself in very deep water. The attorney must be able to cut through all the intentionally confusing mumbo jumbo and get to the meat of any arrangement. Only then is it possible to determine whether or not an artist has a good deal.

When to Get an Attorney

You hire an attorney as soon as anybody wants you to sign a contract or agreement of any kind. The attorney should, in fact, negotiate the management contract on the artist's behalf. No real manager is going to object to the presence of an attorney representing an artist he is trying to sign to a management contract. In fact, he would be wise in protecting his own interests to suggest that the artist get an attorney if he doesn't yet have one.

On the other hand, unless the act is an already established act, it is unlikely that a successful manager is going to permit himself to be jacked around by some attorney. The manager is more likely to say, "Look, here's my contract. It's the same one I've been using for years. I think you should have your attorney look it over, just so that you understand it clearly. But if you want me to be your manager, then you'll have to sign it as it stands. I am satisfied with it, and it's the one I use."

As far as the management contract is concerned, the wise attorney will attempt to negotiate the contract's end, even as he negotiates the signing of the contract at its beginning. The manager will almost always want to keep his percentage of any publishing, recording, or commercial endorsement deals which may have been set while he was manager, even if they continue to exist long after he is no longer the artist's manager. This is usually a point of contention. The manager feels that since he initially arranged the deals, he should continue to be paid for them as long as the artist is making money. The same applies to any renewals or extensions of such contracts or agreements.

The artist, on the other hand, feels that his manager has already been paid, at least up to the point where they parted, and shouldn't be paid beyond that. Any new manager will want to be paid on anything the artist is making from the time that the new management agreement starts, so the artist doesn't want to be paying two managers.

Who's right in this case? It doesn't matter. What matters is the deal which was worked out by the attorneys and signed by all parties at the outset. That is the deal which will be honored, one way or the other. You can't come back and say that you didn't know what something meant several months or years later. Again, you need an attorney before you sign anything.

How to Pick the Right Attorney

So how does an artist find the right lawyer? The Nashville phone book is literally full of lawyers, with over thirty-three full pages of listings. And just because an attorney proclaims himself to be an entertainment lawyer does not make it so. Many so-called music business attorneys derive the majority of their income from non-music-related pursuits. To make matters worse, the phone book reader frequently sees the statement "Tennessee does not certify specialists in the law and we do not claim certification in any listed area."

The best way to find the right attorney is to ask people who are supposedly knowledgeable. Publishers, other writers, and other artists are usually the best sources of information. Get the names of several music business attorneys, not just one. Call and meet these different lawyers. Find out who they have represented in the past and who they represent now. Most importantly, see whether or not their personalities mesh with your own.

The artist needs to be comfortable with his lawyer, because he will be telling his lawyer many things of a highly confidential nature.

During the course of an entertainer's professional life, the relationship with a lawyer may be the primary and most enduring relationship in the artist's entire career. The lawyer may be called upon to hire and fire a manager, negotiate a record or publishing deal, arrange a divorce, handle the purchase of a tour bus or house, get a singer out of jail or out of a lawsuit, and deal with dozens of other situations and circumstances. The potential for attorney involvement in an artist's career is almost unlimited.

Conflict of Interest

One of the most important considerations for anyone seeking an attorney in the music business is the possibility of conflict of interest. Within the music business "conflict of interest" usually means anything which conflicts with the interests of whoever is in charge, or more generally, with whoever is talking at any given moment. What the term is supposed to mean, however, is that one lawyer cannot fairly or adequately represent two opposite sides in the same situation.

For example, a lawyer cannot serve as the lawyer for a record company and at the same time represent an artist signed to that same record company in a matter involving both parties. The same thing applies to managers, publishers, producers, and so on. The conflict of interest might not necessarily be restricted to a particular lawyer, but might involve another lawyer within the same firm who is representing someone on the opposite side of the fence.

While there are thirty-three pages of lawyers listed in the Nashville yellow pages, the number of entertainment specialists is much smaller. The number of really front-line entertainment lawyers is much smaller still. Consequently, there is a great possibility that a prominent entertainment lawyer will likely represent several important clients, from publishers, to record companies, to producers, and anyone else under the sun. What this means is that the individual who has secured a music business attorney may find himself, as a client, being informed by his lawyer that the lawyer can't represent him due to a long-standing relationship with the party on the other side of the fence.

Since there is no way to know whom you will be doing business with next year, or ten years from now, there is no guarantee of safety as far as the selection of a lawyer is concerned. Furthermore, there is no guarantee whatsoever that a lawyer or firm who represents you might not take on a richer, more powerful client in the future, whose purposes might not be in your best intrests. Unless you are extremely rich and powerful, you are subject to displacement in your lawyer's affections at any time by someone who has more money or clout. Hopefully, this will never happen to you, but don't be surprised if it does.

For the artist, the question also arises as to whether it is better to be represented by a smaller but more efficient law firm or a larger and more powerful one. The larger the firm, the more likely the artist will be lost in the shuffle. On the other hand, a larger firm has access to research which a smaller firm would not have. Also, large firms tend to have power, which may be exercised in a client's behalf. The firm an artist chooses, regardless of size, should have an experienced, first-rate litigator in house, that is, a lawyer who fights courtroom battles for a living. Otherwise, if there is a courtroom brawl later, the artist will have to hire an additional attorney or attorneys, while retaining his own lawyers.

Court

With the possible exception of the professional litigator, lawyers don't like to go to court. A lawyer would much rather make a deal and save himself the trouble of many hours of research and preparation. While there are times for lengthy courtroom battles, it's usually best to avoid them. Frequently the results of such battles are unpredictable, and not a question of right or wrong but about winning and losing.

The Attorney as Manager

Due to his knowledge of legal matters, the attorney can, under certain circumstances, be the best manager an artist can possibly have. The circumstances I'm referring to occur when an attorney gives up his legal practice to manage an artist full-time. An attorney who is really in the practice of law doesn't have time to be a lawyer and a manager, and for this reason, the artist should, under most circumstances, avoid hiring an attorney as his manager. Again, there are exceptions.

General Considerations

The attorney faces the same problems posed by the artist as does the manager, the agent, or anyone else. He is subject to the same wild flights of ego and off-the-wall rantings and ravings as any other member of the entertainer's team. While the artist is more likely to respect the observations of his lawyer, the first encounter with an artist's other side is always a sobering experience for the inexperienced attorney. Chances are the lawyer was never subjected to such a display in law school.

Artists frequently have no idea what an entertainment lawyer really does, don't care, and often view his job as no more than a task performed by a clerk. Furthermore, artists are often reluctant to take the time to meet with their attorneys, even though they should, and would rather concentrate their time on more enjoyable pursuits. Add to this the inflated ego of an artist who feels that he doesn't have to take orders from anybody, and there is likely to be a conflict with the attorney, who has his own ego and doesn't feel like humoring an artist just to keep his business.

The successful entertainment lawyer needs to understand the nature of the artistic temperament in general, and the ego size, desires, and fears of the particular artist or artists he will be handling. Artists are often masters at browbeating and manipulating the people who work for them. Their actions can be highly stress-producing for the attorney as well. It is important for the attorney to establish his power, if not dominance, in the relationship.

The attorney's best tool in dealing with any artist is to secure the artist's absolute trust and confidence. If the artist feels that the attorney will always act in his best interests, no matter what, then the attorney's job can be made much easier. Even under these favorable circumstances, the attorney, like other members of the artist's team, is subject to dismissal without reason or notice. If an artist will lie to his manager or agent, he will also lie to his lawyer.

Problems for the Attorney

Artists often feel that they don't really owe an attorney his fee after he has performed his services on the artist's behalf. This can manifest itself in one of several ways. The artist either feels that he has done all the work and doesn't owe the attorney any money, or feels that the attorney has charged too much for his services. The lawyer then has the obligation to explain his fees and is faced with the decision as to whether he will file suit on his client or eat the bill. Neither option is particularly satisfying to the lawyer.

The best way for the attorney to protect himself from his own client is to document his work at every stage. A copy of any written correspondence to anyone should be sent to the artist. If the lawyer makes a phone call or has other conversations regarding the artist, the artist should receive a note detailing what was said. If the artist can see the flow of activity, he is more likely to feel that he is getting something for his money. If, on the other hand, the attorney fails to communicate with the artist on a regular basis, the artist will not know that the lawyer spent three hours on the phone with the record company's legal department. Nor will he know how many contract drafts or redrafts were done by the lawyer.

Having an artist for a client often makes communication difficult for the attorney. Reaching an artist on the road by mail or fax is often impossibile. And even after the artist has returned from the road, there is no guarantee that he will regularly contact his attorney.

Advice to the Artist in Dealing With the Attorney

Don't lie to your lawyer or withhold important facts or information. If the lawyer is not properly armed with all of the necessary facts, he won't be able to help you. It doesn't matter how great the gun is if it doesn't have any bullets. If you don't like or trust the attorney you have chosen, get another one you like better.

As far as fees are concerned, there are often misunderstandings between the artist and the attorney. Part of the problem comes from the fact that most music business attorneys bill by the hour. In any situation where some-one is paid by the hour and not by the job, it is in the best interests of the person receiving the money to take as long as possible to do the work. In many cases, the attorney, cannot or will not tell the client how long a particular job will take. Problems are almost guaranteed to arise.

The situation is similar to having an expensive car repaired. The fact that you are there in the first place puts you at the mechanic's mercy. He says something like "Buddy, I can't tell what it's gonna cost till I find out what's wrong. I can't do that until I get inside the problem, and that's gonna take a while." Either way, count on spending some money.

In addition to spending the money, there is always the fear that the mechanic doesn't really know what he's doing. The same applies to lawyers. While almost all lawyers are expensive, many are much more concerned with being paid than they are with working. Still other attorneys care about their reputations and strongly desire to build a solid practice over a long period of time. In fact, the ideal situation for a lawyer is to represent a client on a continuing long-term basis.

For the artist, the best thing to do is to ask the lawyer in advance what his services will cost in a particular situation. If there are unforeseen complications, the fee will be higher. Also know that while some lawyers write contracts from scratch, the majority of them have a series of standard contracts already on file in their office computers. It's a very simple matter to fill in the blanks or add an extra provision or two in order to customize an existing contract form. In other words, you may be billed for five hours on something which actually took forty-five minutes of applied effort.

If the lawyer will not tell you how much a particular service will cost, at least try to get a specific ceiling. That is, attempt to get him to say that it won't cost more than a certain amount. If that amount is something you can live with, then you've probably done the best you can in the situation. Again, do yourself a favor and find an attorney before you sign anything with anybody.

Jobs

There are many opportunities for a successful career as an entertainment lawyer. Most law firms receive large numbers of inquiries and resumés, but there are two primary questions for any established attorney. Does he need another lawyer working for him, and can he afford to take on another unskilled and untrained attorney? The consensus is that no matter where a lawyer has received his legal education, he's not ready for entertainment law just because he has a degree and has passed the state bar exam. The aspiring entertainment attorney needs to take additional music business classes at someplace like Belmont College or Middle Tennessee State University. Many music lawyers study songwriting, publishing, recording, engineering, and everything else associated with the music business. The music business attorney must understand how everything works if he is to be able to accurately advise his clients.

3

The Record Company

For the aspiring artist, the record company is the most important stepping stone to success, fame, and fortune. Without a record deal, there is no airplay; without airplay, there is no name recognition, and consequently no concert appearances, no merchandising, no product endorsements. In short, no career. For this reason, the aspiring artist must have a record deal with a major record label if he or she wants to becone a country music star. An artist may be popular in his hometown and might be a good singer, but unless the act goes beyond a local or regional following, his real opportunities are limited.

While there are definitely mutual points of interest, agreement, and purpose between the artist and the record company, it should always be remembered that the record company is in business to make money and to show a profit. This all-important fact should be kept in mind by the artist, manager, agent, publicist, and anyone else who seeks to do business with any record label. As mentioned elsewhere, the artist is merely a means to that end. The artist and his music are the product which the record company produces and sells. It could just as easily be pickles or automobiles. The fact that the people who work at the record label may happen to like music is secondary to their overriding purpose—that of increasing product sales.

The record company for the most part knows what is acceptable to country radio, and as a result tries to release product which falls within those fairly narrow programming lines. Every once in a while, the record company is faced with an artist who does not fit within the scope of its overall plans, yet who is too good to be denied. Generally speaking, if an artist is enormously talented but over the edge musically or difficult personally, a record company will pass over such an artist in favor of some good-looking clone the public is more likely to accept. Occasionally the record company suspends its herd signing mentality long enough to support someone who has a voice and who really can sing. But this is the exception.

What the Record Company Does Not Want in an Artist

Sometimes a record company will reject an act because the manager has a bad reputation, that is, someone at the label doesn't like him, for whatever reason or reasons, not necessarily that he is a bad or ineffective manager. Some aspiring artists might shy away from such a manager, when in fact he may be very effective. A yes man is of no value to any artist.

A record company might pass on an otherwise acceptable act because the act has too much baggage in tow in the form of a manager, producer, financial backer, and others to whom the artist might have prior, binding commitments. Dealing with too many cooks can mean more trouble than the artist is worth. So keep your options open. The record company also doesn't want to deal with some artist's half-wit spouse, or anyone else, including the artist, who is going to be constant trouble by, for example, calling employees in the different branches of the record label four or five times a day with suggestions and comments on how they ought to do their jobs.

The record company is also definitely not interested in being involved in any legal battles between the artist and former managers, other record companies, band members, or anyone else. They would just as soon pass on the artist. The label is also not interested in having to deal with any artist's drug, alcohol, or other personal problems of any sort. The record label is not there to serve as a counseling service, legal department, domestic relations adviser, or rehabilitation center. The record company exists to sell CDs and tapes.

An artist who has no individual or defining style is also usually rejected. Today many people at the record labels do not have the "ears" to be able to hear a good voice and decide what needs to be done with it. Furthermore, they probably don't have the time. If the record company is presented an artist as a package, with a unique and specific style, a recognizable voice, and a definite image, the label can either accept or reject the concept. The employees at the record company do not want to figure out which direction the artist should take creatively. This artistic persona should be determined by the artist and his associates long before he comes to the record label.

Getting a Deal

If you can find a creative gap at the record label and fill it, your chances of being signed are much greater. For example, if a record label has four bands, you have a better chance of getting signed if you are an individual singer. If the label has only one woman on its roster, your chances of getting signed will probably be greater if you are a female singer. The record company's roster is available over the phone, so finding out its numbers of male artists, female artists, vocal groups, sister acts, and so forth is not difficult.

There are many ways to approach the record company and many ways a deal is made. A powerful and well-connected music business attorney is one way. Word of mouth is another. There is a buzz about you around town and somebody from a record company decides to check you out. If he likes you, he may bring someone in a decision-making position to see you. Another artist may recommend you to the label. A successful producer, manager, or agent may call someone at the label and suggest that they have a look at you.

Again, here as elsewhere, the emphasis is on *no* rather than *yes*. You would think that the record company would want to sign as many great artists as possible. Why do they pass on so many people? Why are you so much more likely to be turned down by the record label than accepted, and what can you do about changing the outcome in your own situation?

First, let's look at why you may likely be rejected. The laws of inertia apply in the music business as well as elsewhere. An object at rest will remain at rest unless forced into motion through some outside influence. If someone says no to you and passes on you as an artist or writer, then that person's job is done. He can go to lunch or home for the day. He hasn't put his job or himself at any risk by taking any chances, and he hasn't done much work. Furthermore, the record company head hasn't gone out and signed someone who subsequently lost money as a result of his efforts.

The fact is, if you look at the people who have survived in their jobs at specific record labels for any great length of time, it will usually be noticed that these people are not the risk takers in the business. If you don't rock the boat, it is much less likely to capsize and throw you out. From their end, "No" is a complete sentence.

There are several equally important reasons why you are likely to be turned down. One is that most of the people in a position to turn you down are not in a position to sign you. Another very important reason is that nobody really knows who is going to make it and who isn't. We will address both of these situations elsewhere.

What happens when the answer is yes? "Well, he's Jim's new act." Immediately the guy who signed you becomes a target in his own right. Perhaps it would be more accurate to say that suddenly there is a spotlight on him. His name will be associated with you by the people within the record label from that point forward. If you make it and become a star, there will have been so many other people involved by that time, that the person who recommended you in the first place will, in many cases, have diminished in importance due to the influence of others at the label. By the time a new artist's product appears, someone within the record label will have secured a producer or studio time. Someone else will have designed and executed cover art for the project. Still others will have determined a release date for the artist, a marketing plan, record promotion, artist development, and so on.

When an artist is signed, all of these elements come into play, whether the artist makes it or not. Getting a new artist into the marketplace involves a great deal of time and effort on the part of many persons, as well as a great financial expenditure. If the artist doesn't make it, people generally remember who signed the artist in the first place. For these and other reasons, it is easier for someone at the record label to say no than yes.

Whether the coup de grâce is administered kindly or coldly and brutally, a no is still a no. One well-known lesser dignitary at one of the major labels has no hesitation whatsoever about telling an artist, "Your material sucks, and it will never get a deal anywhere in this town, and you better go back where you came from." People who treat artists this way are usually fired. Someone whom they have unnecessarily mistreated earlier moves into a position to return the favor, and does.

The A & R (artists and repertoire) representative at the label is usually the person who signs an artist to a record deal. Most A & R people respect the struggles of the aspiring artist and will gently dismiss you in order not to discourage you or hurt your feelings. Sometimes this is a kindness, and other times it's not. If you have a meeting with someone in the A & R department and have your material rejected, you need to find out why specifically. Usually the person rejecting you will say, "It doesn't do anything for me," followed by something of a more positive and face-saving nature, such as "I like your voice though."

Your ultimate aim is to get beyond no. For this reason, you need to get a critique, if possible, from whomever you are talking to. The person may be an idiot, or he may be very knowledgeable. Either way, he knows something you don't, and you need to get him to respond honestly. You have to let him know that you won't be offended by what he has to say. Then you may receive some helpful advice. Ask him what he's looking for. Was it your voice or your material he didn't like? Does he have any ideas, recommendations, or suggestions about what you should do next? Does he know anybody he might call who could help you? These and other questions offer at least the possibility of getting something out of the meeting.

It's easier in most cases for a new artist to get a record

deal than it is for an established but older artist. Understandably, this fact is discouraging to artists with lengthy and well-established track records as hitmakers. Part of the reason for this sad phenomenon is that the country music business increasingly appeals to a younger audience. Some older acts like George Jones, Waylon Jennings, Johnny Cash, Ray Price, and a handful of others, are regarded as living legends. However, many other veteran artists are simply perceived as old, dated, out of fashion, or otherwise undesirable. From the viewpoint of the record companies, older artists don't sell records. Maybe they don't. One thing is certain, if they are not recording and releasing records into the marketplace, and if their records aren't readily available in stores and being pushed by the record labels, nobody will buy their records. But any artist who has released fifteen or more albums may have already said all he has to say musically.

Probably the main reason that older artists have been pushed aside in Nashville is that the people who run the music business themselves are getting younger as the old-timers die off or retire. The music now being signed, recorded, pushed, and played is more reflective of the tastes of those who are now making the decisions.

Ultimately, for the artist seeking a record deal, the solution to the problem is very simple. It is necessary to have recorded music which is so great that anyone who hears it cannot refuse to recognize it. This means the right voice, the right songs, and the right production. How you look is important, as are your height and weight. Your personality, stage presence, and live performance are also important, and so is your voice. But if the music you present to the record label is not absolutely undeniable, then you are not necessarily going to get signed to a record label.

The New Challenge to the Record Company

While every record company and every artist are desperately seeking airplay, there really are more artists than
there is airtime. The mainstream singers who fit within
country radio's comfortable format will continue to have
an easier time getting played. Often, however, the more
unusual artists keep the music vital and growing. These
artists push the envelope and open the door for other
artists who are also not quite mainstream. These acts are
important to the future of country music.

In the early and mid 1970s, it was the outlaw movement. Artists like Waylon Jennings, Willie Nelson, David
Alan Coe, and others wanted to do things their own way
musically. They fought the powerful status quo and set
creative precedents in Nashville which were unthinkable
at the time, but which artists now take for granted. These
artists by their courage and success made it possible for
many others who followed, artists who otherwise would
have never had a chance to even get signed at all.

The key word here is "success." Had their efforts at
setting new musical and administrative directions failed,
their contributions might have gone unnoticed and country music might have remained unchanged for another
decade. Today nobody thinks of Willie Nelson as an
"outlaw," he's just Willie Nelson. Waylon Jennings has
short hair now, and is just Waylon Jennings. David Alan
Coe is still a bit off the wall when compared to Garth
Brooks, but he is no longer an oddity. These artists and
others made their way, and did so commercially. They not
only opened the door for other artists who would follow,
but they expanded the audience of country music listeners, which resulted in new jobs within all branches of
the industry. For these and other reasons, it is important

that the record companies and radio make room for newer and different artists.

Given the lack of available airtime for new artists, and the resistance to change within the music business, the greatest challenge to the record companies today is to find and develop newer and different ways of introducing artists besides radio. In the future, artists may be able to enter the charts at the larger metropolitan stations only after they have already become famous.

It's like what they say about credit. You can't have credit until you borrow money, and you can't borrow money until you have credit. You won't be on the radio until you are famous, and you won't be famous until you are on the radio. The future challenge for the record companies and radio will be to make room for newer artists and yet retain the uniqueness which separates and distinguishes country music from other popular forms of American music.

The Inherited Artist is Better Off Dead

One of the most unfortunate positions for an unestablished artist to be in is to be signed to a record label and then get caught in the middle of an administration change or a policy shift. If the person who signed the artist to the label has quit or been fired, especially if it's before the artist's first release on the label, the artist is likely to be in serious trouble. Such things happen frequently. When an artist is inherited, or passed down to the new commander in chief of the label, the artist is likely to be lost in the transition shuffle. The new record company president doesn't want to make his predecessor look good. If the artist does not succeed, it confirms the fact that the person who signed him in the first place really didn't know what the hell he was doing. Besides, the incoming label head has his own priorities. In nature, the conqueror often kills the babies of the vanquished. It's no different in the music business.

I managed one artist whose first release on a label coincided with the firing of the label's head of promotion. The head of promotion was a big fan and advocate of the artist and had held that post for nearly twenty years. He left the very day that this artist's first single was released. His replacement was not familiar with the artist, came from out of town, and had all of his stuff still packed in boxes in his office two weeks later.

Needless to say, the record in question proved a disaster, and the label decided not to release another single. The record company released the album but did not promote it. The whole process wasted a year of the artist's life. These things happen, and there is nothing anyone can do to prevent them, especially if there is no advance notice.

Custom Sessions

While Nashville is famous for country music, it's also infamous to a certain degree for thieves and parasites who prey upon aspiring artists and take advantage of their inexperience and hunger for success. These leeches are seldom mentioned, but are tolerated, because they operate within the law. Another reason they are tolerated is because their activities create revenue and feed the system. The most notorious crooks are the purveyors of what are known in Nashville as "custom sessions."

The very term itself is hotly controversial within the music community here. Actually, the term "custom session" refers to any recording endeavor which is not under the auspices of a major record company. Thus a custom session can accurately be anything from a legitimate, union-approved session, to a "scab," or nonunion session.

In a legitimate recording session, a studio is secured, a union contractor hired, and union musicians selected. Whoever bankrolls the enterprise pays the union, and the union in turn pays the musicians. In Nashville, session musicians are booked in three-hour blocks at the hours of ten A.M., two P.M., and ten P.M. The musicians are paid $43.97 per hour for demo sessions. A demo session yields a lesser-quality recording than a master session. The term "demo" is in fact an abbreviation of the nearly forgotten term "demonstration." A demo is cheaper than a master session and is used for a variety of purposes when the highest quality isn't really necessary. For example, a music publisher would use a demo recording to pitch a song to an artist in the hope that the artist would record it.

There is a two-hour minimum required for demo musicians, and the session leader receives double scale, or $87.94 per hour. The employer must also pay an additional fee of 10 percent of the total cost toward the union pension fund and $15.00 to the union health and welfare fund, per man, per session.

A master session is recorded generally for the purposes of broadcast, transfer to cassettes or CDs, or for shopping a record deal. In a three-hour master session, the musicians each receive $263.81 per man for three hours' work. Again, the leader receives double scale. There is a restriction of fifteen minutes of recorded music imposed by the union. In other words, the union won't permit the artist to end up with three hours' worth of music for three hours' worth of pay.

The union also has a special one-and-a-half-hour master session. The cost here is $174.11 per hour for the sidemen and double for the leader. A maximum of seven and a half minutes of recorded music is allowable in this case. Custom sessions have received a bad name outside of Nashville due to the duplicity of a few unscrupulous companies and individuals. *Sixty Minutes* did a rather scathing report on the dirty end of this otherwise legitimate business.

One thing is certain, and that is, if you want to make it as an artist in Nashville, the medium of exchange is recorded material. You must have a tape of reasonably good quality if you want to get any kind of deal either as an artist or songwriter. Getting something on tape is your first priority.

Let's look at the way it generally works in Nashville. Somebody from out of town wants to record an album or a single. The artist finds a producer who offers to assist the artist for a certain fee. Many studios provide an engineer who serves as producer as part of the cost of studio rental. Also, many famous producers regularly work with unknowns as a sideline. If you want to approach one of these, it's easy enough: Look at the credits on an album of an artist whose music you like. Call the producer or production company listed and speak to someone at the office and find out what it would cost for that producer's services on your project. There is no set fee or specific charge. The producer can charge whatever the market will bear.

The producer questions the artist and thereby gains insight into the artist's goals. Does the artist wish to do demo or master quality recording? Does the artist have his own songs, or does he need to get them from publishing companies? How many songs does the artist wish to record? How many musicians and instruments does he want to use? Would he rather use his own band?

The producer can provide help to the artist in clarifying and determining his exact needs. He can recommend musicians, publishing companies, studios, and so on. Again, the more you already know about what you want to do, the more he will be able to help you focus musically.

The producer next determines how much money the artist has available for the project and estimates what the recording session will cost the artist, based upon the information the artist has provided. If the producer and artist agree to terms, a contract is signed and the artist pays the producer a deposit. The producer lines up the studio and the musicians for a specific time, and the music is recorded. It will be mixed or edited and then transferred to CD, cassette, or record, and the project is complete.

The artist returns to his hometown with a record he can sell from the bandstand or play for his friends, and everybody is happy. The producer, studio, and musicians have done their best to make this artist sound as good as possible. Everyone has been paid and all is well. No promises have been made. The artist has not been misled in any way. Everything was clearly spelled out in advance in writing and the contract is there for immediate reference if any specific questions should arise. This is how it is supposed to work, and how it does work in most cases.

The artist, if he possesses any intelligence at all, can call the musicians' union in Nashville and find out what he must pay the musicians. He can call the studio and find out what it will cost. It may sound strange, but some people will come to town and record, then later feel as if they have been cheated, even though they agreed to everything, and nothing was misrepresented. Some of these same people are very vocal in their discontent and consequently to some degree unfairly give Nashville a bad reputation. The artists with the least talent are usually the most dissatisfied.

Now let's look at the same scenario from a slightly

different perspective. Most aspiring artists who come to Nashville hope to become successful and famous. They may say that they merely wish to make a record to sell at home, but the fact is that they secretly hope or even believe that a famous producer might wander off the street into their session, or that an A & R man from a record company will somehow hear their music and rush out to sign them. This overwhelmingly pervasive attitude on the part of all aspiring singers leaves them open for a subtle but effective fleecing.

The custom sessions producer is in business to make money. In order to do this, he must put together recording sessions, ideally as many as possible. Operating under some degree of legal scrutiny, the unscrupulous producer must be more circumspect than in the past. He must choose his words very carefully, and make no false promises, in order to avoid prosecution. The bottom line, however, is that he must close a certain number of deals in order to survive. While promising nothing that is not actually covered in the contract, he can lure the artist into his financial web in other ways.

If the artist is a songwriter, for example, he might say something like, "Listen, this is really very good material. I had no idea that you were this strong as a writer. A good friend of mine runs [and he names some publishing company]. I feel certain that he could use this material. In fact, I think that several of these songs would be just right for [and he names some famous singer]. But let's see what happens. I think that, well, in my opinion, with your voice and this material, you might be able to get a record deal yourself."

He goes on, "We need to get these songs recorded right, with good musicians in a top studio. At that point, after we have a really great tape, I would be willing to call [some well known record company head]. He is a very close friend of mine. I can't promise you anything except that he will listen to something if I send it over. I know him though. He won't even listen to anything unless it is a really good quality master or demo [depending on how much money the producer is trying to extract]."

By such offhand remarks, ringing with little bells of hope, the producer reels in another sucker. This is all perfectly legal and well within the boundaries of the law, despite the fact that it may be unethical.

The next custom session follows the same procedure as the one just mentioned. In this case, more money is involved. The producer again stays just within the limits of the law. He merely offers an extended range of services. He promises to arrange the recording session, have the music mixed and mastered, and a record, tape, or CD manufactured. He promises to mail the record to various radio stations. He may even offer to release the record on his own company's independent label. He tells his prospective client that his label is well known among DJs throughout the nation. In short, depending upon the amount of money that the producer is able to extract, he is prepared to furnish a total package to the artist.

He fails to mention, however, that any record bearing the label in question is doomed to go directly from the radio station's mailroom to the trash bin.

Again, all of this is within legal limits. Since more money is involved, the producer is even more anxious to close the deal. The more services he can provide, the more he can pad the bill. The producer is again performing a legitimate service, one which he knows beyond any doubt will bear absolutely no fruit for his client. Again, the exact responsibilities of the producer are spelled out in a written contract which protects both parties.

There is nothing, however, which protects the client from the false enthusiasm displayed by the producer and his accomplices. The enthusiasm causes the client to feel hopeful about the outcome, even though there is not a snowball's chance in hell of the project's producing anything worthwhile. The producer talks about how the artist can realistically hope to gain recognition in the independent charts and maybe get noticed by "scouts" at the major labels as a result.

The fact is, however, that in the country music business, such things rarely happen. As with other professions, you are either in the major leagues or you are not. There is no in-between.

The next step down is the scab session. The producers of these recordings are the most unethical of all. They will say or do almost anything to ensnare an unwary client. They may use a jerry-built studio, an incompetent engineer, and bad, or at least inexperienced, musicians. They operate outside of the law, often charging exhorbitant sums, and are willing to take their chances of being sued at a later date. They want everything they can get out of each deal now and are not concerned with the future. These producers do not work through the musicians' union, although they may actually employ some union musicians. The system in Nashville allows these people to operate.

There are over three thousand musicians signed with the Nashville branch of the AFM (Musicians Local 257). There are, however, more musicians wanting to do session work than there are sessions for them to play.

With hundreds of new and unknown musicians in town trying to make the big time, there is a shortage of legitimate work. Many times these unknowns will agree to play for unscrupulous producers in order to survive. Often these musicians are members of the AFM. In many cases they are not.

In addition to surviving financially, these unknown

musicians obtain helpful experience in the studio. They are paid less than union scale, but it's usually in cash. Union members who get caught playing these nonunion sessions are subject to fines, suspensions, or other disciplinary measures. But most musicians, union or otherwise, would rather work in a studio for less than union scale than not work at all.

Custom sessions are not by their nature an evil. Legitimate custom sessions do provide opportunities for many artists that would not exist otherwise. It is my experience that in the long run, almost every artist who belongs at the top gets there one way or the other. Most people duped by dishonest record producers bring it upon themselves.

In order to be safe, the aspiring artist should check out potential producers to the best of his ability. This in and of itself is no safeguard. I know of one girl who was charged forty thousand dollars for a project by a well-known producer who didn't need the money and shouldn't have done it. Not only did he take her money, but he pretended to be in love with her and took advantage of her physically and emotionally. He promised her a record deal, but after he collected his money she could never reach him again. It was as if he dropped off the face of the earth. Not an unusual occurrence.

My advice to anyone planning a custom session is to record all conversations with these producers. If they don't have anything to hide, it shouldn't be a problem. The artist should shop around, getting the best deal, and should request sample contracts to read at home, away from the hype of the producers. On no account should an artist sign anything or hand over any money until he has first returned home and thought about the deal at great length.

Many aspiring artists are led to believe that any

hesitation on their part indicates that they are "not really serious about their careers." It is this very seriousness which should cause them to evaluate their options. It is in the producer's interest, not the artist's, to close the deal quickly. So many people come to Nashville and, because of impatience or the expense of hotel rooms and meals, seek to get everything settled while they are there. In the long run, it is more productive and cheaper to make several trips to Nashville than it is to get roped into a bad deal.

4

In the Recording Studio

The modern recording studio is a cool place indeed. The dimly lit control room, the command center of the studio, is much like the cockpit of a jumbo jet or submarine. There are lights, dials, meters, and gauges everywhere. Also, there are rack-mounted amplifiers and playback equipment, like cassette players and compact disc machines. A large boxlike device, which is the actual recording machine, has two tape reels positioned on the flat surface of the machine. At the back of the machine is a display of two rows of lighted gauges, one for each track. The control room is usually smaller in size than the rest of the studio but usually provides a sofa and chairs for guests.

The control room's central feature is a large dial-and-light-covered platform called the control board, console or sound board. This control board ranges in size from two feet wide or less for a home studio to as much as ten feet or longer in an average multitrack studio. Picture the console as a very large desk, covered with rows of vertical knobs from top to bottom and left to right. There are usually two or three chairs placed on one side, facing the control board, like chairs at a desk or table. One chair is for the engineer, another for his assistant, and the third for the producer.

If you are seated in one of these chairs and facing the control board, you will notice that there is a full bank of buttons and knobs extending from you for about three feet, ending at the base of a lighted Vu-Meter. This meter indicates the input or sound level coming into that particular track from one of the instruments or microphones in the studio. The sound comes from the instruments and vocals in the studio directly into the sound board. From the board, it goes into the actual tape recorder.

If there are twenty-four tracks, there will be twenty-four rows of knobs and twenty-four Vu-Meters, one for each track. These rows of knobs are positioned in front of you from left to right across the top of the board and control the volume and texture of the music as it enters the recorder.

Looking forward, past the sound board, you will see a glass wall in front of you at a distance of several feet beyond the sound board. On the other side of that glass wall is the actual recording studio. It is here that the musicians play while recording. The presence of this glass wall enables the engineer and producer to visually monitor what is happening in the studio.

Still seated at the console and looking above the top of the glass wall, toward the ceiling, you will see facing you, in the control room, two very large speakers. The music being played in the other room comes to you through these speakers after passing through the sound board and amplifiers. In some studios, the speakers are hidden in the wall behind a cloth covering and are all but invisible to the naked eye. They are there though, and always positioned in approximately the same place in every studio, above the glass partition, one on each side.

These particular speakers are called studio monitors and usually consist of an enclosure with a treble horn on top and two fifteen-inch speakers underneath. There are two, one on each side of the wall facing the control board. There are two other, much smaller speakers placed on top of the control board, about three feet in front of your face, one at each end, to your left and right.

These small speakers are as important as, and possibly even more important than the larger speakers overhead. While the music coming into the sound-insulated control room through the big speakers sounds rich and full, with searing treble and thundering bass, the fact is that the music must be recorded and produced with the average man on the street in mind. Since the standard car stereo (with the exception of certain parts of California) doesn't possess two fifteen-inch speakers, the producer and engineer must tailor the music to sound as good as possible through these smaller speakers, the type most likely to be found in car radios.

The actual studio part of the studio, where the musicians are located during a recording session, is usually much larger than the control room and most likely has a higher ceiling. Like the control room, the studio has built-in sound insulation from floor to ceiling, so that there are no unwanted echoes or other sounds bouncing around which might interfere with the music. Portable sound baffles, actually padded walls of various sizes, can be moved around at the discretion of the engineer, in order to provide additional sound insulation where necessary. The idea is to make the room as accoustically dead as possible.

Any well-equipped studio will have a grand or baby grand piano, that is, an eighty-eight-key accoustic piano of seven to nine feet in length, and a Hammond B or C-3. The piano must be tuned to the industry standard A 440 pitch immediately prior to each session. Since the piano is an accoustic instrument, it cannot be plugged directly into the sound board but must be miked. Isolated from other instruments, the piano often has its own room, as do the drums. Almost always, you will find a separate room for the singer, especially when the singer will be singing at the same time the musicians are playing. In large studios, there may also be a special place for the string section.

During a standard recording session, the musicians lay down basic rhythm tracks and the singer sings what is known as a scratch vocal. The scratch vocal is more or less a rough practice vocal which provides some guidance for the musicians. The main vocal track, the one which will be on the record, is usually recorded later in the session, after other instruments have been added.

After the rhythm tracks have been recorded, the producer begins to augment the basic tracks with additional instruments. A twenty-four-track studio means that the recording machine can accommodate up to twenty-four different instruments or vocals at the same time, with a particular track being assigned to each instrument. When all of the instruments have been added, the main vocal track and the backup vocals will be added.

When the recording end of the project has been completed, the final product will be roughly mixed and transferred from twenty-four tracks down to a two track configuration onto either a reel or cassette format. This means that the artist, producer, and engineer will set the various instruments and the singer's voice at the best sounding levels for the time being.

This rough mix is like an unedited manuscript for a book. It is fairly close to the finished product, but not quite. There is still time to change or redo any part of the tape if desired. The artist and producer will live with the tape for the next few days and get a feel for it, away from the studio. This is helpful. In fact, it is easy for an artist or producer to get too close to a project and no longer be able to tell what sounds good and what doesn't. It is often wise not to listen to the song or songs for a few days in order to be able to return to the music objectively.

Chances are that if you are reading this book, you are familiar with a recording studio already, but for those who may not be, let's examine it briefly. Any multi-instrument recording like a CD, cassette, or record consists of many different tracks or instruments. The best example of how this works is for you to take twenty-four cards from a deck of cards and place them in a line side by side in front of you, from left to right. We'll call each one of these cards a track. One card can be a steel guitar, another can represent the drums, another the lead singer, another one can be the piano, and so on. You now have twenty-four tracks, each of which represents a particular instrument.

They are all still in a straight line from left to right and side by side, all at the same volume level. We want to turn up the drums, so move the drum card higher than the other cards. Next, move the lead singer's card higher than the drum card, since this is a vocal recording and not an instrumental. You like guitar, so move the guitar card higher than some of the other instruments. Every card will be moved into a different position in relation to the others.

Let's say that you don't need one of the instruments you've already recorded and don't want to use it; bring it back down to the level where it was when you started. If you need another track you can record over this one that you didn't use. When you are satisfied that all of the instruments are at their best possible levels, you can separate the twenty-four cards into two stacks of twelve each. This is mixing them into the two channels you hear in any stereo, the left and right speaker channels. Now place the two stacks of cards side by side, and you have the finished tape. This should give you an idea how tracks work.

In the old days in the studio, when a recorder only had one track, music was usually cut live, with everybody playing at once, as if the artist was actually performing on stage. If the finished product didn't sound good, or an instrument was out of tune, or the singer off-key, or somebody played too loud, the song was recorded again. If it still wasn't right, it would be rerecorded as many times as necessary until the artist and producer were satisfied. Whichever was generally agreed to be the best recording of several takes would be the one which was finally selected for the actual record.

Some artists cut live today, following the old format and having most of the musicians there at the same time, as if they were actually performing. When this is done, each instrument is assigned its own track, unlike in the past. For most artists, it is much easier, for most artists, and ultimately less expensive to spend some time playing with the various tracks after they've been recorded. This is called mixing.

The fact of the matter, as any producer knows, is that many who pass as singers can't really sing that well, or in some cases, at all. The producer will record the instruments, dispose of the musicians, and then go back into the studio and privately, away from everyone else, literally piece together the song line by line, and in some cases, word by word, with the singer singing a piece here and another there on several different tracks.

The producer will then select the best parts of several vocal tracks and mix them onto one track. The finished product will be as close to perfect as it can be, and in most instances will sound better than the singer could ever make it sound singing the song live, straight through nonstop, beginning to end.

This is cheating in a sense. A singer should be able to sing without having to resort to technical trickery to record a song. On the other hand, the singer is doing all of the singing, and it is his or her desire to provide the public with the best possible product. The practice exists and is widely used.

There are other recording techniques which are generally unknown to the public. The speed of the tape machine can be increased or slowed down to change the pitch of an artist's voice. The singer's voice can be doctored with other effects such as reverb, or echo, which give it a depth which it doesn't possess in real life. Many of these effects have been employed in recording studios for years.

Producers and Engineers

In addition to the artist and musicians, and a bunch of well-wishers and hangers-on, the recording studio always contains a producer and an engineer. The producer is perhaps the most important person in any artist's career in terms of the songs one hears on the radio. The producer's role is to connect the singer and the song in the best possible way. If the singer has got what it takes, then the producer will work to place the artist's particular and unmistakable imprint on the song. If he has succeeded in his job, he will have produced a hit song.

The engineer primarily deals with the technical aspects of the recording. He is truly a technician in every sense of the word. He knows every piece of equipment in the studio, inside and out, not only how to get the best use from each one but how it works as well. He knows how the various pieces of machinery interact with each other, and can usually repair one of them if something goes wrong.

During the recording session, the engineer sets the volume levels for the various instruments, determines the placement of microphones and musicians throughout the studio, and operates the board while recording is in progress. He also operates and monitors all of the equipment in the studio, such as the actual tape machine, via the transport controls. There would be no recording whatsoever without the engineer. The engineer also usually maintains the studio where he is employed and keeps the equipment cleaned, calibrated, and in a constant state of readiness.

There are different schools of thought concerning the relationship between producers and engineers and the function of each. One group holds that before anyone can be a producer, he should first be trained as an engineer and should possess the technical know-how to run the board and every other aspect of the recording studio. How else can he get the sounds out of the artist and equipment that he seeks? There is much to be said for this view, and many successful producers in Nashville did in fact start out as engineers. It would seem logical that the more technical knowledge a producer possesses, the more effective he would be at getting optimum use of the studio, its equipment, and ultimately the artist.

Others feel that technical knowledge of that sort, while desirable in theory, is not really necessary in fact, and can in some cases actually detract from the producer's ability to do his job. The theory here is that the producer is a music person. His work and the flow and groove of the session will suffer if the producer has to stop what he's doing and rearrange microphones and musicians or fool with other technical problems in the middle of a session.

There are truly great producers in both categories. In the future, as more colleges and universities provide a musical curriculum, chances are that the successful producer will have had extensive technical training as an engineer somewhere in his background. Be that as it may, it is also likely that during an actual recording session, the two will retain their individual roles in much the way that a pilot and copilot fly a plane.

Producers connect with artists in many ways. The record company may suggest a producer, an artist may choose a producer, or a producer may solicit an artist. Many times a producer, like a manager, will become involved with an artist only after the artist has already become established. Ideally, a producer finds an unknown act, works with him, nurtures him along musically, takes him to the record label, and gets him a record deal.

Some people within the industry feel that the artist and producer should approach an album project with the intention of recording ten number one absolute smash singles. Others feel that if an album has three smash or hit singles, that it is going to sell a certain amount anyway. There is no point in wasting ten really great songs on one album. Each album should aim for several hits which will propel it to high sales, and the rest of the album should more or less be filler. By spacing ten hit songs over a four- or five-album span, the artist and the record company will, in theory, sell a great many more records. Later the best hit songs of several albums can be combined for a greatest hits album for even more sales.

On the other hand, if an artist is aiming solely for hit radio singles, he is likely to pass on certain songs which do not fall within that format, yet which are important in defining his overall status as a singer or songwriter. An example would be a song or songs dealing with subject matter which is more or less irrelevant to the eighteen-to-twenty-five-year-old listener. An artist's music, however, can't be all fluff; there must be substance as well. Ideally, there should be enough A sides (hit singles) in an album to sustain an artist at the level of radio for a year to a year and a half.

There are many ways for a producer to handle an actual recording session. Each situation is different. In most cases, the producer selects the musicians he intends to use and then chooses and books the studio for a specific date. The material which will be recorded is often selected by the producer, and sometimes by the artist. It is usually more of a collaboration between the two which determines the actual songs to be recorded. The entire musical flow of the session itself depends upon the artist and his own ideas and sense of direction. Many artists possess clearly defined opinions about their musical careers, and are right on track. In instances like this, the producer becomes more of an accessory than an orchestrator. Often, however, an artist has no idea what he needs to be doing musically, or has wrong ideas, in which case the producer will become more of a musical guide and director.

When the producer feels that the artist is off track, it is his duty to express his opinions. Despite what they might say, many artists are often not interested in opinions contrary to their own. They want to do what they want to do and don't care what anybody else thinks. The potential for a real conflict between the producer and the artist in such cases is very high. In a standoff of this nature, who's right?

If the artist records music which he doesn't like, or is forced into a musical direction which doesn't fit him or isn't in keeping with his image, he stands to forfeit his career. Since the music business today is radio driven, an artist is constantly under the gun to record hit singles. If he follows someone else's advice, knowing that he does so against his will, two things can happen. If it turns out that the artist was wrong, and by following the producer's instincts a hit single is cut, then the artist and everybody else is happy. On the other hand, if the artist permits his own instincts to be overridden and it turns out that the producer was wrong, then the artist's career may also be in serious jeopardy. Is it better for an artist to fail following his own instincts or to fail following someone else's? Neither scenario is particularly appealing.

Here, as elsewhere, honesty should be a fundamental business principle. The producer should stick by his guns. A producer who permits himself to be trampled by the artist isn't doing the artist any favors. Sometimes a producer just gives up because he has other things to do and doesn't feel like arguing with some artist. The producer is getting paid anyway. If the artist wants to cut bad music, let him. On the other hand, music is a subjective thing, and often the artist really does have a direction, which may seem obscure at first, but which, if followed to its conclusion, may succeed. When differences of opinion exist within a creative situation, the key is for both sides to attempt to be as open as possible.

No doubt some successful art dealers and critics did not care for Picasso's work, and surely a so-called expert must have told Salvador Dali that dripping clocks were not an appropriate subject matter for an artist. In Nashville most successful artists were passed on by several record labels. Perhaps the artist should have his chance, and if he is a true artist, the final product will reflect his art. But then, many people within Nashville aren't interested in talking about art. Some wonder privately whether art is even possible within the existing format. Basically, what we're talking about is cutting commercial and radio-friendly hit records which sell. Art may evolve as an accidental by-product.

In the studio, there are different types of producers.

Some are slow, methodical, and technical, while others seek to capture the magic of the moment. Still others yell and scream and keep everybody on edge, feeling that true music can only come from turmoil and chaos. Often, producing is about 40 percent music, and the rest, an effort at keeping people on the same wavelength long enough to get a project completed. There is no set way which is right or wrong. Yet music is supposed to be fun. Most of the producers I spoke with, or have seen working in the studio, were there to produce hit records. That was their primary objective. If a producer is able to come up with hit records, how he does it is not really important.

The greatest thrill a producer can have, from a creative standpoint, is to take an unknown song, bring it to life with an artist, and hear the song become a hit on the radio and be accepted by the public through record sales. And yet the question sometimes arises in an almost metaphysical sense, how much does a producer really contribute in the case of an artist like, say, Elvis Presley, Roy Orbison, or the Beatles? Aren't these artists so great that it wouldn't have mattered who produced them?

Maybe so, but in the case of Roy Orbison, producer Fred Foster was a definite and contributing part of the magic, since Roy Orbison had few hits after they stopped working together, even though his voice didn't change throughout his life.

The same question may be asked about an immortal song. While it's true that songs like "Somewhere Over the Rainbow" could have become hits with nearly anyone singing them, the fact remains that Judy Garland was the singer who had the hit with that particular song. While many artists feel that they are the geniuses behind their success, the fact is that anytime a hit song is produced,

there are always a number of factors involved which are peculiar to that specific time, place, and situation.

The artist is obviously a primary element, but then, so is the song, and so are the musicians. One guitar lick at a certain spot in a song, for instance, may become the song's signature. Roy Orbison's "Pretty Woman" comes to mind. The psychological and emotional vibe at the particular moment a hit song is recorded is something which exists at precisely that moment, and may have been the most important aspect of all. It cannot be duplicated. Ideally, the chemistry between the artist and the producer results in a creative combination which is greater than the sum of their collective abilities.

The only constant in the music business is change, and this is true for the producer as well as the artist, and everyone else who is part of the system. In order to stay on top, a producer must constantly look for new projects which will either be a part of the current trend or lead into the next one. This is a real dilemma for the producer because like artists, producers can become obsolete. There are many famous producers with incredible credits in Nashville who are no longer even considered by the record labels or current artists for upcoming projects.

What dangers does the producer face? Over and above the possibilities of obsolescence all music people experience, there are few natural predators, enemies, or other dangers confronting the producer. In fact, there seems to be an overall feeling of fraternity, and the belief that when one country music producer is coming out with hit songs, his success helps country music in general. While this is not universal, the level of cutthroat competition between producers seems far less than that which exists in other parts of the country music business. With as many artists as there are, there is enough work for everybody. The

producer's relationship with the artist follows much the same pattern as the agent's or manager's. There are some artists who display great loyalty, while there are others a producer can't trust out of his sight.

One negative aspect of record production which everyone admits exists but which nobody claims personally to have been involved with is the situation in which a producer forces an artist to record songs from the producer's own publishing catalogue. This usually happens to inexperienced artists, but it can theoretically happen to any artist. For example, a publisher has a song that several artists want to record, because everybody knows it's a hit. The publisher could offer the song to a specific artist with the provision that the artist do one or more additional songs from the publisher's catalogue. The artist might counter with, "I'm willing to do that in order to get the song I want, but I want half the publishing rights on the other songs from your catalogue which I decide to record." Any deal is possible regarding publishing, producing, and songwriting.

Writers can be exploited in a different way by a famous artist, and often are. The artist says, "Hey, look, I'll cut your song and put it on my next album, but I want half the writer's credit, or part of the publishing, or both." For the writer, the question then becomes, "Is it better to have a hundred percent of nothing, or to have this famous artist cut my song and be forced to give up half of it?" The answer depends on the writer's confidence in the song and in his own abilities.

How is a producer paid? The producer usually receives a recording budget from the record label, which includes a fee for his services. In addition to this up-front money, the producer will receive points, or a certain percentage of each tape or CD sold. While every deal is different between the record company, the artist, and the producer, they almost always are similar in that there is an advance and points. The producer, like the artist at the record label, makes his money from volume sales. If a product doesn't sell well, the producer doesn't make much money.

The Ending of the Artist-Producer Relationship

The artist's relationship with a producer usually ends because the producer fails at some point to come up with hit records for the artist. In some cases, the album or singles may reflect the artist's best work but fail to make their mark for other reasons. For example, somebody at the record label considers the artist to be a low priority and doesn't push the project to make it successful. While the music itself may have been great, and the artist acknowledges that the producer was not at fault, he may feel that the producer is jinxed anyway and choose someone else for the next recording project.

Another reason the producer and artist part ways is that during the course of several successful album projects together, they have exhausted their creative powers. They may simply have gone together as far as they can. Nobody is right or wrong, it is simply mutually agreed that the artist would likely do better with another producer.

At other times, the successful artist may begin to feel that he knows more than any producer possibly could about his own musical goals, and may dismiss his producer and decide to produce himself.

While there are other reasons that artists and producers split-up, those listed above occur most frequently.

The rule should be, If it ain't broke, don't fix it. If a producer and artist are consistently having hit records, there is no reason for the artist or record company to bring in a different producer.

Jobs

One of the best ways for anyone interested in becoming a producer to start out is by getting a job at a music publishing company. By working in that environment, you will eventually have an opportunity to produce demos on the songs in the publisher's catalogue. This experience will teach you how to produce songs quickly and cheaply, as well as how to operate the equipment. These demos are pitched to artists and producers around town in the hope that an artist will record them. Eventually someone, whether artist, producer, or A & R man, will ask who produced the song. If you show a flair for combining an artist with a song, you will eventually come to someone's attention. If you place yourself in the loop, by networking and extending your contacts, you will get an opportunity to prove yourself and show what you can do. Don't expect recognition and reward overnight. You will have to pay your dues like everyone else.

Is the art of record production an inherent talent or something which can be learned? Some people feel that a true producer is born and not made. Others hold the opinion that it is a profession which may be learned by anyone willing to spend the time it takes to become an expert. Either way, the job of producer is one of the most interesting, challenging, and rewarding in the music business.

5

Record Promotion

Record promotion is one of the most important jobs in the music business. Record promotion means pushing a record, talking it up to various important people, such as station managers, program directors, and consultants, and getting the record played on the radio.

One record promoter defined record promotion as "servicing radio." By this he meant giving radio the product it needs, providing the station managers with research, visiting them, helping them with promotions, and so on. Without airplay, the greatest recording in the world will never be bought. If nobody hears a song, or an artist, then there is no awareness of the artist and no public demand. No record product sales, no concert dates, and no merchandising. In short, no career.

Besides advancing the artist's career, many other unspoken interests and priorities occur at the same time. The record company wants hit artists who sell millions of records. Within the record company itself, there are publicity and artist development people, marketing personnel, record company executives, accountants, and A & R people, who all want to advance their own careers.

Simultaneously, competing radio stations seek a larger share of the listening marketplace, so that they can get more advertising revenues. There are station managers, program directors, and disc jockeys, all wanting to further their own careers and feather their respective nests. Also, music publishers seek to build impressive and valuable song catalogues.

Others who have a stake in the artist's success include record producers, studio musicians, recording studios, engineers, managers, talent agencies and agents, auditoriums, road musicians, and others. The artist is the vehicle for all of these people and their various dreams. The success of the artist and all of the people in supporting roles depends on radio airplay.

The Charts

All of the promotional efforts of the record company, the independent promoters, and a host of others are directed toward the specific end of getting a record radio airplay and top chart position. A chart is essentially a printed list stating a particular record's popularity at a given time, within a given area. The area encompassed by the chart can be local, regional, or national, depending on whose chart you are looking at. The higher a record's popularity, the higher its position on the charts. In a sense, the charts are to a record what a blue ribbon is to a show horse. A top chart record indicates to the industry and to the public that the artist is a valuable commodity. This value becomes tangible when it translates into product, merchandise, and concert ticket sales. For these and other reasons, a top chart record is something to be greatly desired by all parties involved.

Needless to say, some charts are more important than others. The most important charts nationally are produced by *Billboard,* Gavin, and *R & R (Radio and Records).* These charts and others would appear to mean little to the average listener in radioland. However, what happens with these charts does determine to a large extent what listeners will hear on the radio at local, regional, and national levels. These particular charts are very important to those people whose livelihood depends directly or indirectly on an artist's success. An artist's position on these charts not only indicates the amount of airplay an artist receives, but also causes other stations to either add or remove that artist from the playlist.

Billboard magazine provides an on-line computer subscription service called BDS, which stands for Broadcast Data System. BDS is an electronic tracking service, which monitors 147 reporting stations at the time of this writing, twenty-four hours a day, seven days a week. A reporting station is a station which due to its ratings strength, or popularity within its area, has been selected to report its daily and weekly playlist to *Billboard* magazine through BDS.

Each song played on the radio is encoded with a special and unique signal which is picked up and monitored by a computer, which counts and records how many times that particular record is played in the top one hundred markets in the nation. The number of plays a record receives nationally through the BDS-monitored stations determines that record's position on the national *Billboard* country singles chart. There is no guesswork involved, the tracking system is monitored airplay, accurate, and purely objective. A spin in New York City counts the same as a spin in Pascagoula, Mississippi. As a result of this modern and extremely high tech system, it is no longer possible for powerful individuals to manipulate the charts in their own favor.

R & R has 216 reporting stations and selects its reporters in much the same fashion as *Billboard*. It seeks the stations with the highest ratings in a specific geographical region. The number of reporting stations varies, from a low of 150 to a high of 230, within the past twelve years. Like *Billboard, R & R* may have more than one reporting station in a particular city, and it also may have reporting stations which also report for *Billboard*.

One significant difference between *Billboard* and *R & R* is that while *Billboard* concentrates specifically on the top a hundred markets nationally, *R & R* concentrates on the top two hundred markets, thus reaching deeper into the heartland of America. While *Billboard* creates its weekly charts from electronic program monitoring, *R & R* physically calls each of its 216 reporting stations every Monday morning. These stations tell *R & R* the specific songs they intend to play in the coming week, what songs they plan to add, and how many times they intend to play them. So the *R & R* chart is based upon projections of what a station expects to play in the forthcoming week, while the *Billboard* chart reflects what was played the week before.

R & R's chart is always a week ahead of *Billboard*'s. On the other hand, *Billboard*'s charts are 100 percent accurate, whereas this is not the case at *R & R*. In other words, a station might fully intend to play a certain record twenty spins per week, but might actually play it fewer than twenty times, or even possibly more. Frequently subscribers compare the two, seeing how close they mesh. *R & R*, while lacking the high-tech methodology of BDS, should not be considered any less of a player. Its reports are relied upon and considered to be extremely important.

The third player in the charts game is Gavin. Formerly known as the *Gavin Report*, Gavin, as it is now called, is a San Francisco–based company with weekly charts in all fields, from country to urban. Gavin has approximately 207 reporting stations in the country field, and produces a Top Fifty country singles chart. Like *Billboard* and *R & R*, Gavin has stations in major markets, some of which also report to *Billboard* and *R & R*. Gavin, however, reaches deeper into the local markets than *Billboard* or *R & R*. This is a significant point, in that some of the stations in smaller markets have a less rigid playlist and are more likely to give a new artist airplay than larger stations would. For this reason, many believe that Gavin is the best place to break a new artist, that is, to get the artist some national chart recognition.

Gavin does not weight stations. The term "weight," in this context, refers to the practice of considering one particular market or station more important than another. For example, in a weighted situation, a play in Dallas would be more important than a play in Elephant Butte, due to difference in population base and station power. Gavin operates on a point system, depending on the number of plays, with a variation for light, medium, and heavy rotation. When a song receives a certain amount of points, it enters the Gavin chart. Gavin relies on phone calls from reporting stations to establish its weekly charts. The chart is faxed to subscribers on Monday night, and the report is mailed on the following Wednesday. The mailed report contains editorials, record reviews, charts, and information relating to all musical formats.

So how do the three major charts rate? That depends on whom you ask and on what you ask. The fact is, all are different, unique, and important.

The average person has at one time or another heard the expression that a song is "fifteen with a bullet," or "ten with a bullet." Regardless of the number, the term "bullet" refers these days to upward chart movement. The actual designation may be an asterisk, a star, or an underline, depending on the publication, but the generic term "bullet" means that a record is advancing, based on radio airplay. On the other hand, the term "anchor" means that a record is moving down and out of the charts.

Frequently in the past an artist would have a so-called hit record which didn't actually sell well. Such records were referred to as "paper hits," since the only place they existed as hits were on charts, and not in the real world. How could this happen? How could an artist have fifteen number one records in a row, yet sell very few actual records at the retail level and have very poor ticket sales at clubs and concerts?

Stations would report that they were playing a record, when in fact the record was not being played, or at least not being played to the extent that the station reported. This was done basically for the purpose of humoring record company personnel, who in some cases were more interested in high chart numbers than in reality. Another frequent problem in the past would be that a record might be number one on one major national chart and number fourteen on another. Many felt that certain charts were being manipulated.

That such things no longer happen is due principally to the advent of BDS and SoundScan, two accurate electronic methods. BDS reports actual airplay numbers, and SoundScan logs actual product sales numbers.

Record Promotion

So how does a record get promoted? An artist delivers his finished product to the record company, usually in the form of a fully mastered digital audiotape. The tape is translated into CD singles, which are then sent to the major market reporting stations by the record labels. These singles are for station use only, and not for sale to the general public. The other approximately twenty-four hundred country radio stations receive new product every other week from a company called CDX.

CDX is a Nashville-based company which fulfills a strategic marketing service for the major record labels in Nashville. Every two weeks, CDX releases a new CD and mails the CD directly to the majority of country radio stations nationwide. The CD is multilabel, and contains all of the new single releases from all major labels, combined on one compact disc. The record labels tell CDX which songs to include and provide master tape, label copy, and other information.

The CD is printed up and mastered alphabetically, according to song title, placed on one disc, and shipped to the stations. A major label can release as many songs, or as much other information, as it wants. A record label might also include station i.d.'s and interviews on the CD. At this time, there is room on any CD for a maximum of eighty-two minutes of programming. If more broadcast time is required, CDX is prepared to release a second disc to accommodate the overflow.

This procedure certainly simplifies the singles release problem for all concerned. The radio station is saved sifting through dozens of individual packages and is assured of receiving the top country products in digital broadcast quality, twice a month. Furthermore, the stations don't have to call the labels constantly, requesting new products.

This method helps the record companies, since they do not have to constantly keep up with the ever-changing number and location of radio stations nationwide.

Until recently the twice-monthly CD allowed space for only one independent label song. The rest of the space was devoted solely to Nashville's major labels' new releases. Starting in March 1995, CDX removed the one independent label song from the major label disc and started a

second disc consisting solely of independent label releases. This additional disc features up-and-coming artists on independent labels and is entitled *Showcase*.
Unlike the major label disc, this CD is released once a
month. No major label artists are included on this disc,
and the service is available to any independent label at a
cost of $1,368 per song.

The artist is excited about having finished his work
and is anxious to see it hit the charts as soon as possible.
He may have spent months working to get it just right. But
not every record is immediately released into the market
by the record company, just because the artist has
finished a project. The record company has many artists
and must schedule its product releases in such a way that
each artist will get the best shot at getting the most
possible airplay.

Record promotion, as a rule, is handled locally, at
branch offices within specific geographical areas of the
country. PolyGram, for instance, has nine regional promotional branch offices. Not all record companies have
that many. There are, however, certain key markets recognized by all record labels as desirable for record promotion. These markets are always areas with or near a high
population base, and are considered essential in terms of
establishing a hit record. Some frequent market bases for
regional branches include Detroit, Chicago, Dallas, New
York, Los Angeles, Atlanta, and Miami.

If the record company is a large one, there will be
several separate categories of music represented at each
branch location. For example, a regional major record
label branch office is likely to house a separate promotional person for each department of the label, for example, rock, pop, country, classical, and urban. The regional
field staff are the backbone of the record promotion
business. They are responsible individually for what goes

on within their own designated regions. There they have the autonomy to get the job done, and there is little danger that someone else from within the label's promotional staff will get in their way or duplicate their efforts.

The regional people are expected to know more about their stations than anyone else and are supposed to be the experts on the list of stations they are given by the label's director of promotion. They are expected to visit the stations and know the people there as well as become familiar with their personalities.

Over and above the various regional promoters are the national directors of each branch. For example, the various regional and local promotion people answer to a department head, who is based in Nashville, in the case of country music. The head of promotion works within the label's overall promotion budget, plans strategy, and fulfills other duties. Promotion heads do not as a rule make calls which would interfere with the work of their staff in the field. They might, on the other hand, work with some of the larger national accounts as programming consultants, a subject we will examine later in this chapter.

Within each branch are sales representatives, who act as the company's local salespeople. Then there are account service representatives, known as ASRs, who visit retail accounts and persuade store managers to devote a certain amount of space to their record company's artists. If an artist gets no rack space, there will be no product sales. A rep might try, for example, to get a retail outlet manager to put up posters or large displays promoting a new product release on a particular artist. Public awareness leads to product sales. Obviously, one of the most significant jobs of the director of promotion is to lobby the record label for as many field people as he can get.

The record promoter's main job is to call designated

radio stations within his particular region to persuade the station manager or program director to add a desired record to the playlist. Right now there are almost three thousand country radio stations, but that number increases constantly due to changing format. In other words, country music is extremely hot right now, so a station's management and ownership might decide to cash in on the increasing popularity of a particular type of music by switching over from one type of music to another, in this case, from something else to country.

Radio stations set aside specific times each week when promoters may call and make their pitch. These are known as call times. By setting aside certain hours on specific days solely for that purpose, the station manager or program director permits himself the opportunity to pursue a regular work schedule. Otherwise, the sheer volume of calls would take up all of his time. With the promotional staff of nearly twenty country record labels and dozens of independent record promoters calling weekly, it is easy to see how a station manager could easily be overwhelmed.

A typical call to the program director from a record promoter could go something like this; "So-and-so's new single just entered the charts this week. We're gonna go for breaker [get the song in the charts for the first time]. We've got some good phone stories happening on this record. In Lubbock they're playing it thirty-eight times a week. It's on in Chicago, Dallas, Milwaukee. The singer is scheduled for *The Tonight Show* next week. He's going on a twenty city tour opening for so-and-so. The stations are getting a ton of phone calls from females. It's a good female record. The sales are up in your market, the album's Top Fifteen nationally. I really need your help in breaking his new single. You know him, you've met the man. He's a good guy, and this new record is great. Help us out."

Sometimes the promoter will not push the record directly, preferring to offer the illusion to the program director that the call is of a more conversational nature. The call is to find out how the record is doing. In this case, the promoter might hear that his record "is getting good phone action," meaning that listeners are calling the station and requesting the record. The promoter can use this information and parlay it to his advantage with another station.

Many times a single or album will be doing very well nationally but for some reason a station will not play it. This is obviously very discouraging to an artist and to the record promotion man as well. Frequently, by citing actual sales figures from important stations in other areas, the promoter can persuade a station manager to begin playing a record. The sophisticated record promoter today has all the information he needs in a computer right on his desk for easy access. Through a number of subscription services, he can pull up the top two hundred albums, check the sales of albums and cassette singles, and retrieve other information quickly. There are, for example, ninety-nine ADI markets, that is, local sales markets. The promoter can access SoundScan, the *Billboard* service which provides actual sales figures on a number of products.

At other times, sales figures are of no consequence, and neither are reports from elsewhere in the country. Some stations just simply will not play a record. Period. For example, a prominent Washington, D.C., station refused to play the Kentucky Headhunters' first record, stating that they thought the act was too rock and that it didn't matter who else was playing it.

While making phone calls can be extremely important, getting through to the program director and getting
the desired results are more important still. For this
reason relationships with key people in radio are actively
sought and developed by record company promotion
people and independents alike. One of the best ways is for
the artist and record promoter to visit the station. These
visits are usually planned in conjunction with the release
of new product. A good time to apply a concentrated
effort in this direction is two months prior to the release
of product.

Another significant aspect of record promotion, especially at the beginning of an artist's career, is the live
performance. Enabling the radio people to place a name
together with an artist's face is obviously very important.
Consequently, live performance showcases are usually set
up in specific regions, hitting major record market areas,
prior to or in conjunction with new product release.

Showcases generally work as follows: Key radio personnel within the targeted region are invited to a show,
generally at a smaller but currently trendy club. They are
provided with drinks, fed, given an opportunity to meet
the artist, and then treated to a live performance. Hopefully, at the end of the night, the DJs, station managers,
and program directors will know and come to love the
new artist's music.

There are many deadly pitfalls awaiting the new artist
at these showcases. The main danger, of course, is that if
the artist has a poor live show, much more harm than
good can result. Hopefully, much time and attention have
been devoted, prior to these showcases, to the development of an artist's live show, as well as to his overall
persona as an entertainer. If the artist comes off badly, it
would have been better for him not to have been seen at
all. The same is true if the artist lacks conversational

skills or is a jerk personally. After all, these showcases are, in most cases, the artist's first introduction to radio people in the area.

Nonetheless, despite the dangers, the showcase is a risk that must be taken. If the artist is successful, no faster route to radio exists. This is show business, and everybody in radio, from the station itself, to the manager and program director, down to the lowliest DJ, is out to make a name for himself. If a new artist really has superstar potential, it reflects well on the radio stations and individuals who were able to recognize this talent early in the game.

The arrangements for these regional showcases and in-person visits to radio stations are usually coordinated between the artist's management, the radio stations, the talent agency, and the record company. A tour bus or air fare is provided by the record company, and the artist and promotion people spend a couple of weeks doing live performance showcases and visiting station managers and program directors at their radio stations. One major label record promoter told me that he visited a total of two hundred different radio stations last year, with five different artists.

Some stations have internal rules which prevent DJs from attending showcases. In these cases, the artist will visit the station in person, meet everybody, and play four or five songs. Again, the goal is to hit an emotional note with the program director. Most program directors tend to be male. Sometimes you try to include some of the women from the station in the session. If you can get a couple of women into that conference room, you've got a much better chance of selling that program director on the act, because he can immediately see their reaction. Females drive country radio. Women aged twenty-five to forty are the most desirable demographic for radio. They are the ones who buy product. It is said that more than 70 percent of all country music sales come from this group.

Here, as in every other branch of the music business, relationships are everything, and are often the determining factor between success and failure. In the case of radio airplay, this is certainly true. With a limited amount of airplay available, getting played is the objective. It stands to reason that a program director, given the option of playing one of five or ten records in a given slot, is going to give precedence to an artist he likes. This is just human nature. The same applies to the record promoter. The program director, all things being equal, is going to be much more likely to play a record for a promoter he knows and likes, rather than one he doesn't know or one he knows but doesn't like. Furthermore, the development of a relationship with a program director makes it possible for the promoter to call the station at other than the designated weekly call times, something a newer promoter would be unlikely to risk doing.

There are about twenty country labels in the marketplace at the time of this writing. These are not fly-by-night labels intent on fleecing someone, but legitimate labels operated by people who have achieved some measure of success and respect in their fields. In the old days, a record could come out of nowhere and have a much better shot at becoming a hit, if it was a good record. Nowadays the competition for airtime is so fierce that it is really difficult to have a successful release, no matter how good it is, if that artist has not performed before a group of radio people. It is imperative that the artist gets around and meets as many radio personnel as possible, leaves as good an impression as possible, and gets a buzz going.

There is a ton of networking going on between radio stations. They talk to each other, and they have little cliques. While full-page ads in the major trade magazines and outdoor billboards are important in their own right, ultimately there is nothing more important to the fate of a record than the word-of-mouth discussion that occurs between program directors.

Record promotion, within the record company itself, has become more part of long-term overall artist development package than a matter of record promotion on a particular product. As the music business expanded and grew, the commitment level which the record company traditionally made to a new artist seemed to diminish. Until recently, country music had always been considered the backwoods cousin of uptown rock and roll. A country record which crossed over to the so-called pop charts was something to be greatly desired and bragged about.

During the late 1970s and early 1980s, there was an exodus of country artists to the West Coast, beginning with Dolly Parton. They wanted to distance themselves from the hillbilly image. Record companies in Nashville began to adopt a West Coast rock-and-roll philosophy of artist signings and product releases. The philosophy was perceived by the record companies to mean releasing a large number of new artists. The more bullets you shot, the better your chances of hitting the target. What this meant for the aspiring artist was that he was under pressure to succeed faster, since the record label was much less committed than in the past.

For the artist who finally thought he had it made when he got a record deal, the results sometimes proved devastating. An album and a couple of singles were released. Nothing happened, and the artist was dropped from the label. It seems that this trend is finally coming full circle, and a much greater commitment from the record label to the new artist now exists than in the recent past. With more commitment, there will be fewer signings per label. This bodes ill for the aspiring artist. On the other hand, there are more labels now than there were in the past. But then, there is only a certain amount of airtime available. So there you go.

A great deal of good material falls by the wayside even after it has been released. Hence the need for and attention to artist development as part of overall record promotion.

Independent Promoters

In addition to a record company's in-house promotional staff, independent record promoters are also usually hired to promote records. Rates vary, as do the inner workings of each company, but promoters are normally paid $200 a week, or a flat fee of $2,500 to $3,000 to work a record, for the life of the record. The "life of the record" is generally considered to be twelve to fourteen weeks, for a hit record. A record which isn't a hit can die quickly, often within a couple of weeks. Many companies require a ten-week minimum, that is, $200 a week, for at least ten weeks. In other words, if the record lasts only four weeks, you are still stuck with a bill of $2,000.

Independents are usually hired by the record company, often as many as three different independent promoters per record. But independents may also be hired by a music publisher, the artist himself, or the artist's management. In fact, some labels expect the manager and the publisher to hire additional independents. It would seem, with so many people trying to push an individual record, that there would be a great deal of duplication of efforts. Indeed, this sometimes happens, but the theory in record promotion is that the more people promoting a record, the better it is for that disc. As with every other branch of the music business, quite a few people engage in this line of work and claim to be experts, but the actual number of independents with real clout at the of major market country radio level is less than a dozen.

Why would a record company hire an independent record promoter when it already has a paid in-house staff for that very purpose? The fact is, while most record promoters have the same contacts, not all of them have the same relationships with those contacts. As one industry insider told me, certain independent promoters are frequently hired as a form of protection, that is, they can hurt you if overlooked. If you don't hire them, they could work against you. But mainly, the prevailing philosophy is overkill. Also, some radio stations feel that they are getting a more objective and therefore more accurate opinion about a record from an independent as opposed to a label promoter.

Also, different independent promoters have individual specialties. One promoter will concentrate on working Gavin stations, while another might devote the majority of his efforts to *Billboard,* or *R & R.* With nearly three thousand country radio stations, there is plenty of work to go around.

Despite many misconceptions, the independent promoter does perform a very definite and vital job for the record company. In ideal circumstances, the independent promoter serves as an extension of the record company's promotional arm. The significance becomes obvious as we examine the regional promoter's job. The record company's regional promoters have a very hectic day-to-day schedule which, in addition to making phone calls to stations throughout their respective regions at specific call times, includes staff and strategy meetings, the coordination of artist showcases, and in-person visits to regional stations.

Given the time taken up by these activities, the independent promoter offers welcome relief. There is no way that even the most diligent record company promoter is going to be able to cover all of the important radio stations in his area. There are 147 *Billboard* reporting stations, 216 *R & R* reporting stations, and 207 Gavin reporting stations. Even though these numbers are divided into geographical areas and assigned to different individuals within the record label staff, the workload is still incredible.

The independent promoter is on the phone five days a week, generally between the hours of eight-thirty A.M. and six P.M., doing nothing but making calls to radio stations. The "indy" works all day everyday, persuading station managers and program directors to add, keep, or advance a record on the station's playlist.

What about conflict of interest? It would seem that with record promoters pushing several different artists' records at the same time, a conflict of interest would arise in that some artists might receive preferential treatment at the expense of other artists. This is certainly a legitimate concern for any artist with a new record out. The priority any record receives is determined within the hierarchy of the record label itself. The label's record promoter is told which records should be mentioned first, which need a bigger pitch this week, and which to pay less attention to.

Here as elsewhere, the squeaky wheel gets the grease. The artist's manager needs to spend time at the record company making sure that it is his artist that receives the big push. Record companies like managers who come forward and ask, "What can I do? How can I help? What can I provide?" So many managers just show up and say, "Gimme, Gimme, Gimme. I want all of this for free." It's refreshing to the label when an artist's manager steps in and offers to help in any way possible. This attitude reflects well on the artist.

This potential for conflict would seem to be bad enough within a record label, but it is even worse with an independent promoter, who might be working several different records for different record companies at the same time.

There is really no way to monitor the independent promoter, that is, no way to be certain that he is pushing the record enough, or that he is even making calls at all. It is rare, I am told, for an independent promoter to phone somebody at the record company and report a record has been added in a particular market, before anybody on the promotional staff at the label knows about it. The record company always knows first. There are, however, incentives and bonuses structured into the pay plan. In other words, the independent promoter receives a bonus if the record reaches the Top Ten, and an additional bonus if the record reaches number one.

Despite what might appear on the surface to be a conflict of interest, the record promoter flourishes. It's not unusual to find several of the Top Ten records worked by the same promoters. Several records may be worked at different levels at the same time by a promoter. Fortunately, not all records require the same level of service at the same time. For example, when the station has just received a new record, the promoter might just ask the program director to simply familiarize himself with the product, in preparation for a large push later on. With a second record, however, the promoter may be pushing for Top Twenty chart position, while with a third record, he might be trying to get it to number one chart position.

The majority of successful and long-term independents are also careful what records they agree to promote. Most look at the records they have agreed to promote within a specific time slot. If the promoter has too many records scheduled to begin that week, he might elect to pass on an offer to promote a record.

Who pays for the independent promoters? In most cases, the initial cash outlay comes from the record company. Some or all of that money is charged against the artist's accounts receivable, and the artist ends up ultimately paying most of the bill out of his share of product sales. As with almost every other facet of the music business, this arrangement is negotiable.

Part of the problem of record promotion within the record company is handled by scheduling product releases in such a way that the artists on an individual record company roster are not competing with each other. There is enough competition on the charts for artists without having to compete within one's own label. Record companies will schedule the simultaneous release of artists who are on its label but not necessarily in competition with each other. An example would be releasing simultaneous product on a hat act, a vocal group, and a female singer, as opposed to, say, releasing three records at approximately the same time on three hat acts. Furthermore, the record company will release different types of records, say a ballad and an up-tempo, simultaneously on different artists, making it possible in theory at least, for the radio station to use both records.

The release date for new product is determined by a mutual agreement between various persons at the record label itself. A staff meeting among the department heads, including sales, marketing, and promotion people, determines what the best time to release a new product will be. Is there any TV planned around the time of the release? What about the accompanying video? Is it ready to go? It should appear a couple of weeks before a single is shipped, so that listeners can start calling the radio stations and create an advance demand. Are any touring dates planned? Is the artist scheduled to work in any major markets? Is this a new artist? Is this his first release? Is it someone who is in great demand? These and other questions influence the date at which a new product will be released.

But scheduling is also important for other reasons. A glut of artists with new product scheduled is like a long line of airplanes waiting on the runway for takeoff. Record companies frequently pass on artists they might otherwise have signed if it weren't for the fact that the label's releases are stacked up and backlogged.

How do the promoters feel about the records which they pitch? Most of the ones I spoke to are not particularly concerned with the music. It is all about numbers. How do they feel about artists? The general comment was that the artist was insignificant other than to the degree that his name helped or hindered the movement of the record. The record promoter's chief concern is promoting the record, not the artist. I spoke to several promoters, mainly independents, who said that they had never even met most of the artists whose records they promote.

Ultimately, independent promoters are a part of the cost of doing business, and are budgeted as such. Like every other group of players in the music business, some do better than others. Some are in great demand. Then, for no particular reason, a new hot favorite person or company moves ahead for a while. Much has been said about independent promoters, both good and bad, but it is likely they will continue to exert a major influence in determining the music America hears on the radio.

Video Promotion

Record companies do not, at the time of this writing, have a promotional department for videos, but there are independent companies who promote videos. The outlets for country video are somewhat limited at the moment, mainly to TNN (The Nashville Network) and CMT (Country Music Television), with an occassional Country Countdown on VH-1.

Consultants

Programming consultants are an increasingly powerful, and some would say evil, influence in the field of radio programming today. The first consultants made their appearance in country radio around 1980, but consultants did not really become a force until the mid 1980s. Essentially, the programming consultant is paid a fee by the radio station for his services, which consist primarily of designing a playlist for the radio station. Theoretically, this list will include better programming and result in more TSL, or time spent listening, to the station which employs the consultant's services.

It is a popular and widely held misconception, even in Nashville, that the consultant dictates the hiring station's playlist, and that this is his full role. If such were the case, the question naturally arises, why would a station in Illinois hire a consultant in Mississippi? Or vice versa? And wouldn't a station's own program director know more about the musical tastes of his own listeners than someone in another state? The theory is that if a consultant has a successful list of radio station clients who have increased their market share, then the consultant should be able to increase another station's business as well. For example, the consultant can analyze a station's current playlist and make suggestions, such as playing a certain amount of oldies a week, and can even recommend specifically which songs to play at what time of the day.

But let's examine the role of the programming consultant in a little greater detail. That the consultant determines the playlist for its clients is an oversimplification of the consultant's job. In fact, while creating the weekly playlist is a continuing part of the consultant's role, there is much more involved.

Most consultants are initially approached by the radio station owner seeking to improve ratings in their own listening area. The consultant meets with the station owner and usually suggests that the station hire the services of an outside research company in order to find out the radio station's real position within the community.

The research company does a market analysis of the station, at the station's expense, determining the station's strengths and weaknesses. For example, a station with fourth-place ranking in a four-station market would be considered weak. The research company also does perceptual studies within the specific area and determines the local public likes and dislikes. It should be mentioned that the research company is not connected in any way with the consultant.

The consultant examines the research report and then formulates an all-encompassing plan which analyzes everything from format, to playlist, to personnel. The plan which is developed by the consultant is individually tailored to each station and is the result of much research. The recommendations include setting up a real team of employees who will effectively move the station forward. The consultant analyzes the individual members of the radio station staff, from the station manager and program director right on down the line, including the station's marketing staff and disc jockeys. If changes need to be made, they are recommended by the consultant.

Part of the consultant's continuing role is the preparation of a weekly report which not only suggests the station's weekly playlist but makes other programming recommendations as well. The suggestions made to the station regarding the playlist are the result of much work and research and reflect the reports from other stations across the nation as well. The analysis is purely objective and almost clinically accurate.

The downside is that the consultant's suggestions are not made on any subjective level at all. They don't play a record among themselves, decide that they like the music, and recommend that it be played. A problem exists for the listener in the sense that no consideration whatsoever is given to the musical merits of any particular record. It is not about music at all. It is all about numbers and the generation of numbers. The consultant might as well be recommending a stock purchase. If there is anything objectionable about the role of the consultant, it would be that someone who has such a major impact on the music which the public hears should have so little relation to it subjectively.

Ideally, a consultant can put together a team which will make the station a winner. The consultant is also on top of things as far as the addition of new titles to the playlist is concerned, and being in a position to add a particular record to a block of stations at one time is certainly an enviable position from a power standpoint.

From the standpoint of the record promoter, the consultant can be a big fish to land or a big problem. Since some of the consultants determine playlists for as many as a hundred or more stations, they can be very powerful and influential. For this reason, they are heavily courted by the record companies. If a consultant, for example, refuses to add a record, a significant part of the public market can suffer.

One of the reasons consultants flourish is due to the real estate value of radio stations. As radio stations have become more and more expensive, the owners have become more conservative and want to hedge their bets. They do this by bringing in so-called experts. According to the head of promotion at one of Nashville's major labels, "We are breeding a generation of program directors who are not learning how to think for themselves. That's the real danger with consultants." What she meant, is that station program directors are, in many cases, becoming too reliant on statistical information instead of listening to the music. They have reached the point that they are only looking at numbers. Ultimately, however, the proof is in the pudding. If the programming consultant's suggestions have worked, then the station's market share in its respective area will show a marked increase.

One last point regarding consultants. A program director or station manager can frequently use the consultant as a scapegoat to get a record promoter off his back, by saying something like "Man, I love the record personally, but we are paying the consultant for his expertise, and we have to follow his recommendations."

Jobs

The best jobs in record promotion go to people who have a background in radio. Entry-level jobs within the record label, however, usually consist of clerical positions and minor duties such as working in the mailroom. These jobs, while seemingly inconsequential, lead to other job opportunities. If an employee handles his duties well and is sharp, sooner or later his work will attract the notice of someone who will give the employee greater responsibilities and opportunities.

In Nashville, as elsewhere, one thing leads to another. The main thing is to be in the loop, regardless of your entry-level position. It stands to reason that an employee insider is much more likely not only to find out about openings within his company but to be considered first for upcoming positions. Also, by being on the inside track, an employee often hears about openings in other related fields.

People with backgrounds in radio make good record promoters themselves. In the first place, most disc jockeys have pleasant-sounding broadcast-quality voices. In addition, most of them are able to speak and communicate quickly, assets which are important when speaking on the phone. Also, the fact that they have been involved in radio makes them sort of unofficial members of the radio fraternity. A natural affinity exists between the promoter and the radio representative if the promoter has a background in radio.

Also, the former program director or station manager is likely to have heard every possible pitch which a record promoter could possibly make. He remembers the techniques and methods which worked on him. Consequently, he is able to call upon that knowledge and experience to make his own sales pitch more effective.

Ultimately, for the person seeking a job and a career in record promotion, the best thing is to get any job you can at a record label or with an independent promoter and work from there. The promoters I spoke to said that the most important qualifications for prospective employees were a good phone voice, communication skills, and above all else, a love of the job and a positive attitude.

6

Radio

The importance of radio to a country act cannot be overstated. The single record, via country radio airplay, is still the main vehicle capable of breaking a country act. While there are nearly three thousand radio stations playing country music at the time of this writing, there are only about two hundred today which really make any difference. These are the reporting stations. Their acceptance of an artist is the only thing capable today of taking a $1,000-a-day-act to a $50,000-a-day-act.

Understandably, the importance of record-fueled, radio-driven singles places an incredible amount of pressure on the artist to cut hit records. The country acts of today which have become household names without hit records can be counted on the fingers of a one-armed man's missing hand. In country music, artists are generally recognized by their hit singles.

While this has always been the case to some degree, the majority of really successful country artists who have passed the test of time may be immediately recognized by their styles and voices. There is no mistaking Patsy Cline, Ray Price, Hank Williams, Willie Nelson, Johnny Cash, Waylon Jennings, Ronnie Milsap, George Jones, Tammy Wynette, Brenda Lee, and a host of others. There are also many great artists who have emerged in the past ten years, such as John Anderson, Reba McEntire, and so on, who will be the immortals of tomorrow. And radio airplay has been the primary means through which these artists have been introduced to the public, and by which they have remained in the public eye.

While video, as a fairly recent entry into the country music field, is certainly important in advancing and sustaining the careers of country music artists, the fact remains that radio is the prime mover. Radio, not video, is being listened to on the job, in the car, in the over-the-road trucks, in the portable units carried by runners and cyclists, and elsewhere. The country music consumer is tuned in to radio. At the parts counter, in the machine shop, and in all areas of the blue collar work force, country music is blasting over the airwaves of radio.

Until the last ten to fifteen years, radio was the only way a new artist's career was started. This has changed for some formats as the result of MTV, but as far as country music is concerned, radio is still the primary marketing tool.

But before we look at country radio, let's look at country music. What is it today? Many in Nashville and elsewhere believe that country music today is really nothing more than evolved pop music. In other words, many feel that country music in the traditional sense really no longer exists, that it has lost its twang and rough edges. More likely, country artists in the thirty-five-and-under range have been influenced by a wider range of musical styles than their predecessors, including everything from the Beatles to disco. These influences have made their way into the music.

Country music as a popular radio format originated as an outgrowth of the famous barn dances of the 1930s, and the barn dances determined what country music would be from that time forward. These early barn dances were variety shows and featured vocals, instrumentals, and comedy. This is especially true with the Grand Ole Opry, the most famous and successful of all such live radio broadcasts. The black musician De Ford Bailey and comedienne Minnie Pearl are classic examples of the variety format. The idea for country music as a genre was to offer a little something for everybody. Country music, more than any other musical format, has been true to its original premise. Look at the present diversity in musical styles encompassed under the banner of country music.

So the statement that country music has changed and is somehow no longer country is partly true and partly false. Country has evolved and changed as America has changed. It has grown along with the population and has been introduced to many outside influences during the last sixty years. This was especially true during World War II, when people from rural and agricultural backgrounds were suddenly thrown together in the armed services with members of the urban culture. When the war was over and those who survived went home, they carried these outside influences home with them. This realignment of values quickly manifested in the nation's music.

As the internationally recognized home of country music, Nashville has itself long been an example of this diversity. Beginning in the 1950s, artists like Elvis Presley and, subsequently, Roy Orbison, Brenda Lee, and others recorded here. Their records, while not considered country, were in many instances embraced by country fans and radio alike. Other artists, such as Roger Miller and Marty Robbins, were considered country but easily moved into what was then known as rock and roll. Nashville has continued to be a recording center for artists in all musical categories and, as the home of country music, has further established the openness of country music as a format to a wide variety of musical styles.

Country music includes such diverse, unusual, and bizarre acts as k.d. lang and Lyle Lovett, as well as R & B–influenced performers like Ronnie Milsap and T. Graham Brown, western acts like Ray Price, honky-tonkers like George Jones, traditionalists like Ricky Skaggs, and cowboy artist Michael Martin Murphey. Add to this stew a shaker like Billy Ray Cyrus and vocal groups ranging from Alabama and the Statler Brothers, to the Mavericks, the Texas Tornados, and Sawyer Brown, and the diversity of country music becomes truly evident.

The same applies to the female side of the genre. Dolly Parton, while considered country, is an international superstar, as a performer, a country vocalist, a writer, and an actress. Within the rank and file of female country artists will be found acts as divergent musically and socially as the aforementioned k.d. lang and Dolly Parton, folk artists such as Mary-Chapin Carpenter, and classic female traditionalist greats like Tammy Wynette and Loretta Lynn. Country music has become the mass-appeal main music format for the 1990s.

Part of this success is due to the increased marketing skills of people now pushing the format. A pop market mentality definitely operates in Nashville now, which takes advantage of marketing plans and skills for the most part developed elsewhere. Furthermore, the increased access to video and other mass-market outlets has made the artists and the format of country music even more popular.

So what does all of this mean to the aspiring artist or to someone seeking to enter radio? At least from the artist's standpoint, country music still offers more opportunities for musical diversity than any other form of popular contemporary music. Consequently, and in light of the increasing popularity of the format, an artist should not be afraid to attempt a career in country music just because he or she doesn't necessarily fit into a specific musical framework.

The Radio Personality

There is one in every town, the disc jockey who does much more than just play the records. He is usually the one you find by accident, channel-surfing on the way to work one morning. He's usually upbeat, nearly always funny, often irreverent, and ultimately the one you listen to. The radio personality is the radio station's star attraction and is a performer himself. Many disc jockeys seek to elevate themselves to this status, and some succeed. For those who do, the possibilities for financially rewarding work in the field of radio are endless. On the other hand, if a radio personality is not really able to engage the listener completely, he merely ends up interfering with the music, alienating the audience, and causing whoever is within the sound of his voice to move up the frequency scale.

When Will a Radio Station Play a Record?

Ultimately, there are only a few reasons why a station will play a record. A record will be heard if it's already a hit, if the program director believes that it will become a hit, or as a favor to someone. In the life of every record, it reaches the play-or-pass level at the radio station. If the program director is "significantly convinced" that it will be a hit, he is willing to take a chance and the record gets played. Ideally, playing a record wouldn't be that big a deal. It's not as if the world will come to an end if a record is played and nobody much cares one way or the other. This, however, isn't usually the attitude at radio stations, but it should be. The station which isn't strong enough to survive playing some good records which may or not subsequently become hits, isn't really that strong to begin with.

This Isn't Us, and It Isn't Country

Many times a program director or station manager will hear a new song or a new artist and immediately and arbitrarily decide on the spot that he isn't going to play the record and that he doesn't like the artist. His likely excuse is "It's not really a country record, and it doesn't fit our programming format." This happened often with the Kentucky Headhunters, Billy Ray Cyrus, and others who subsequently had major hit records. Chances are that these decisions were not based on whether or not the music was country, but upon the personal prejudices of the individual program directors who might not have liked the way the act looked.

When the station manager still refuses to play a record he passed on which subsequently becomes a smash on country radio nationally, it becomes obvious that he is no longer defending his station against the onslaught of heathen music, he's defending his position or, more likely, his ego. As has been established already musically, and has been discussed privately behind closed doors in Nashville, "Most of this shit ain't country anyway." This being the case, the radio stations need to ultimately let the public decide what it is and whether or not they like it. Country music definitely has evolved and changed over the years. The result is that it has gathered and encompassed a much wider listenership than it ever had before.

While this may be alarming for the purist, the public

doesn't seem to mind. This being the case, radio programmers need to be more open in programming and should avoid comments like "This ain't country." The fact might be that at this moment in time very few people really know what country music is, and this includes everyone from record company executives to country radio programmers. And as far as playing new artists and new music is concerned, what fails to evolve becomes extinct.

The Radio Job Market

Why do people want to get involved in radio as a vocation? There are several general answers to this question, as well as a number of particular ones. Many persons enter the field of radio out of a desire to be around music. Others are fascinated with the concept of being able to address thousands of people at the same time over the airwaves. Some are impressed with the technical and operational aspects of radio, the expensive and sophisticated equipment. Still others are performers, possibly frustrated singers, entertainers, or comedians, who view radio as a creative outlet.

There are numerous opportunities within the ever-expanding field of country radio. While there are many colleges and universities with broadcast courses included in their mass communications departments, there is no substitute for experience. One of the best possible ways to gain valuable on-the-job experience is to work at a station in a smaller market. The opportunities presented by the smaller stations are many. You can be a disc jockey, read and write the news, learn about engineering, and work at developing your on-the-air personality. Every small town has a radio station, and the chances of getting an entry-level job are excellent, certainly better than at a large metropolitan station.

While there seems to be some disagreement on whether radio personalities are born or made, all agree the successful radio jock exhibits an extroverted personality. It may manifest itself early in life in the form of good communication and conversational skills, an ability to tell a story or present facts in an interesting way. It's more of an aptitude than a specific type of voice per se. According to the experts, the best advice is to get started early if you want a career in radio. Actually, a high school student should start working at a local radio station on weekends and during summer vacation.

The people who run country radio are for the most part helpful and encouraging and would likely take anyone sincerely interested at a young age under wing and help him or her along. Such experience gathered early gives the student who will be taking broadcasting courses in college a practical advantage which will place him far ahead of students who have never been inside a radio station or who have yet to appear in front of a microphone.

The person who is able to engage a listener over the airwaves in a one-way conversation is truly an artist, and like singing, the art must be honed and fashioned through experience. The best at radio never stop working on the development of their craft, always seeking to improve their broadcasting skills.

Country Radio Broadcasters, Inc.

Country Radio Broadcasters, Inc., is a not-for-profit educational corporation which was formed primarily to promote the art and science of country radio. It has no membership, as such but is governed by a board of directors. Country Radio Broadcasters offers scholarship grants in the field of broadcasting to worthy canditates. Is best known nationally for its presentation of the annual Country Radio Seminar which is held in Nashville each year in late February or early March.

The Country Radio Seminar is a multiday gathering of those who are concerned with radio and broadcasting, both as a source of income and as an art form. The 1995 Country Radio Seminar (the twenty-sixth), for instance, took place at the Opryland Hotel in Nashville during March 1–4. Many of these functions, addresses, and cocktail parties were sponsored by companies such as BMI, Gaylord Entertainment, TNN, the Country Music Association, R & R, and other private and public companies.

The Country Radio Seminar provides an opportunity for old friends with similar interests from around the country to get together, meet and greet, and discuss matters of importance to those involved with every aspect of country radio. The theme for the 1995 Country Radio Seminar was "Taking It to the Next Level." This topic served as a backdrop for the various panel and session discussions centered around that topic, which were conducted and moderated by a wide variety of industry professionals from different fields within the music community.

Some of the discussions included Radio and Music Law, Play to Win, Protecting the Franchise, The Ratings Game, Ratings Versus Revenues, Talking Country, Broadcasting and Marketing, Better Commercials, Fire Up Your Playlist, Managing Sales for Profit, and other topics of interest and importance to those involved in radio. The sessions and discussions were punctuated by luncheons and performances by some of the new and upcoming country music acts, with a special performance by country star Tanya Tucker.

7

The Musician

The musicians bring country music to life. They keep the beat, play the melody, and color the performances of the individual vocal performers.

If you want to make it as a musician in Nashville, the first thing you need to do is join the American Federation of Musicians, known as the AF of M, the AFM, or the musicians' union. Anyone can join.

All recording sessions of any consequence, such as record label sessions, are conducted according to union rules. This means that musicians are paid a specific minimum per hour, work in specific time blocks, and so on. All TV music must also be performed only by union musicians. While recording studio and television work for musicians are conducted according to union mandates, the musicians' union is not an employment agency and does not offer to provide, or seek to find, jobs for musicians.

The musician faces many of the same problems encountered by anyone else seeking fame and fortune in the music business. Many musicians come to Nashville thinking that all they have to do is let the word get around town that they are here, and everything will fall into place. It seldom works this way. The fact that someone was well known as a great guitarist in his hometown does not mean anything in Nashville. Being an exceptional musician is the minimum requirement for consideration.

The aspiring country singer faces an incredibly competitive world, and yet there is no comparison between the obstacles faced by the musician and those faced by the singer. The musician has it much tougher. There are over 1,700 guitar players alone registered with Local 257. In fact, the Nashville local branch of the AFM has the largest number of members in the country, with a total membership in excess of 3,500. Much of this is due to the increased popularity of country music and the subsequent influx of many musicians who are not really country but who have come to Nashville to be where the money is.

While these newcomers are generally accepted, their presence is often a sore point with musicians who were playing country when country wasn't cool. This is understandable, since many of these incoming musicians couldn't make it in other music fields and, in some cases, don't even like country music.

So how does an aspiring musician get his big break in Nashville? As mentioned previously, much of anyone's success in country music depends upon the contacts he establishes and the relationships he is able to build. This isn't something which can generally be done overnight. The musician who is new to town must first let people know that he's here and available for work.

The best way to do this is to start networking with other musicians, writers, publishers, and artists. These people are easily acessible at various writers' nights and other functions throughout town. Writers' nights and open mike nights are specific nights at local clubs where anyone can perform newly written songs. These are gathering places for musicians, artists, and songwriters.

The *Tennessean, Banner,* the *Nashville Scene,* and other local papers and magazines list all of these places regularly. Meeting and connecting with others at these places will help the new musician become known.

The fact of the matter is that session coordinators, leaders, and producers will not hire unknown musicians as long as established and successful players are available for scale. At the same time, getting known won't matter much if the aspiring musician isn't prepared when the opportunity to prove himself arises.

Being prepared means owning the appropriate instruments, being available for work, and possessing a high level of proficiency on the instrument of one's choice. In fact, the musician who is skilled on several instruments increases his odds of finding regular employment. The musician also needs to be versatile in terms of his playing skills and should be able to draw from a wide variety of musical styles and disciplines in order to deliver anything a session or performance might require.

Being able to read music has become much more important as the music business in Nashville becomes more sophisticated, and musicians who read will eventually dominate the market. For now, almost all recording sessions are mapped out according to a number system which is fairly easy to decipher.

What is the life span of the professional studio musician in Nashville? In other words, how long can a musician who is at the top, in terms of demand for his services, remain there? There are several answers to this question, depending upon whom you ask. The studio player with a career in excess of twenty years is rare today, but some do exist. In the future, those with lengthy careers at the top will be rarer still, because of the increasing number of new musicians constantly arriving in Nashville.

In this sense, the studio musician is subject to the

same laws of gravity as the singer. Whatever goes up must come down. Unlike the singer, however, the studio musician will not appear on stage generally, and therefore will, to a certain degree, be exempt from having to be young, handsome, and physically fit. Be that as it may, the studio musician and, to a lesser degree, the road musician are subject to the same laws of career decay that the singer faces. Why?

In theory, at least, a musician should get better with time, should become a better musician with practice and experience, that is, until he is literally too old to play any longer. But many studio musicians who dominated recorded music twenty or thirty years ago in Nashville are not even playing at all now. One possible reason is that the artists they backed up and recorded with are no longer recording. Many of the producers who preferred them are also gone.

The newer producers have their own favorite musicians, as do some of the artists. There is also the sad fact that in Nashville, experience does not necessarily count for much. This is true in most branches of the music business, but especially so for the musician. There is always some hot new player whom everybody wants to use for a while, until he too is replaced.

When are most recording sessions done? People tend to think of musicians sitting around the studio at all hours of the night with cigarettes hanging out of their mouths, being kept alive by coffee, beer, and whiskey. The fact is that while some sessions do run late into the night, most recordings are done during the day, for the simple reason that union scale late at night is time and a half.

Recording sessions occur at specific times, at ten A.M., two P.M., six P.M., and so on. In Nashville, sessions are run in three-hour blocks, so session times have been established which allow musicians who are playing multiple sessions during the course of a day to get from one to the other with relative ease.

The studio musician may well be booked for the entire day at the aforementioned time blocks by one artist or producer. Sometimes a ten P.M. session is booked, but it is likely to wrap up around midnight. At other times, when there is a large budget involved, the record company may book the musicians for four sessions a day for a week or longer. In these cases, the musicians may not actually be used for all of the hours they have been booked, and may spend a great deal of time just sitting around waiting. They are paid the same whether they play or not.

So far we have been looking mainly at the studio picker, and while there are some similarities, the road musician usually lives a different life altogether. The road musician, who is a backup player or sideman for an artist, usually starts out at the bottom and works his way up the ladder. Chances are that, like the singer, his interest in music developed early in life. He probably played in a band in high school or college, or most likely began working as a musician full-time as soon as he got out of high school.

By the time a sideman reaches Nashville, it's likely that he's already done a lot of time on the road, and most often at the lower end of the scale. Most singers and their bands pile into a van or camper to reach their shows, often with a U-Haul full of equipment in tow. Riding long distances in a full van can be very uncomfortable. Often the musicians will share driving duties and will have to unload, set up, and reload their equipment in addition to playing their music. For the unknown artist, it's likely that he will have to do four or five shows a night, usually between the hours of nine P.M. and two-thirty or three A.M. It is not an easy life, but one which most performing musicians are familiar with long before they reach Nashville.

On the other hand, the road musician at the top end of the business has a pretty good life. His motel and hotel rooms are usually paid for, he gets a per diem allowance, doesn't have to set up or tear down, load or unload any equipment, and is transported on a large bus or in a plane. When show time comes, he steps into the auditorium, plays, and leaves, sort of like an expensive hired gun. Most professional touring musicians seem to like their work, especially at the upper end of the spectrum. They enjoy playing before large crowds, like the prestige of being associated with a top entertainer, and enjoy hanging out with other musicians. The long rides between cities are often tedius, and sometimes the hours are long, but it's not a bad lifestyle.

The usual mode of transportation for the country artist is the tour bus. Most buses are large and are laid out pretty much the same. There's a lounge at the front section of the bus which contains a sofa, several chairs, a kitchen of sorts, and a table. There is also always a television, a videocassette player, and a complete stereo playback system. The kitchen is equipped with a small refrigerator, running water, and usually a small stove of some type.

Walking through the front section of the bus, the visitor will pass through a door into the sleeping section of the bus. This usually consists of several racks or thin beds stacked on each side of the bus, generally two or three deep. As you continue down the passageway toward the rear of the bus there will be more beds on each side of the bus, as well as a bathroom, a shower, and storage space.

Eventually you will come to another door. Beyond this door is the artist's stateroom. It is the second largest room on the bus, after the lounge, and usually contains a small double bed, a chair, and a small sofa, as well as closet space, a television, and a sound system.

The successful country artist is likely to operate several buses. He might have his own private bus, a separate bus for his band, and a third bus for his crew. The bigger the ego, the more buses the artist is likely to use, since he will be carrying a larger road crew.

When the artist's fame drops, so will the number of buses he has on the road. While he is at the top, however, the more buses the merrier, especially as far as the band is concerned. It isn't unusual to have eleven or twelve people on a bus under normal circumstances.

For the sideman with greater ambitions, the road, while a necessary part of one's curriculum in the school of hard knocks, is ultimately a dead end. The musician who aspires to be a full-time studio musician can't play in a recording studio while he is a thousand miles away from Nashville riding in a bus. The same may be said, to some degree, about the musician who plays six nights a week in some lounge or club cover band. He may be getting by, but it's like treading water. You aren't drowning, but you're not getting any closer to the shore. Yet riding with six or seven people in a crowded van and sleeping on top of speaker cabinets, or playing cover material in some joint for a bunch of drunks, is all part of average musician's basic training.

The Band

It's now time to look at the band, not as an act like Alabama or the Kentucky Headhunters, in which all of the players are stars, but the band hired to back up the star. The backup band is a combination of individual musicians, which, as a whole, is greater than the sum of its parts. As such, the band seems to develop a consciousness and will of its own, as if the combination of, say, five individual members combines to create a sixth and separate entity. It is this entity which must be reckoned with by the artist.

In almost every band, there is someone who is the quiet, studious type, another who is highly opinionated, another who is there to just do his job, still another who seeks to use the renown of his association with the artist to pick up girls. Add a whiner and a troublemaker. This is a fairly accurate cross-section.

Trouble with the band can come at any time and is usually the result of problems and dissatisfaction stirred up by one or more individual troublemakers. A typical scenario is for the band to threaten a strike on the eve of departure for a long tour or to otherwise create problems at an inopportune moment. Most musicians are usually hired individually, one at a time, as replacements for departing band members, and as such, generally do their best to try to fit in. Some get the big head and start thinking that the artist and the band—in fact, the entire show—can't make it without their services. Generally speaking, troublemakers usually self-destruct or get weeded out before they can create too much havoc. Often, though, as in other branches of the music business, the troublemaker can take others down with him.

The availability of drugs and women invariably appeals to the young traveling musician, but for the picker who has been on the road for twenty years, his interests are likely to be different. The veteran musician is likely to be married and settled down, and wants nothing more than to play, to be paid for his services, and to return home safely as soon as possible.

The musician who wants to work the road with established big-name artists will do well to remember that the artist who has hired musicians to work with him on the road is the boss. The musicians work for him, not the other way around. The musicians are not the star and don't have any rights to make demands of any kind. They are told the rules when they are hired, and their pay is discussed at that time. If any musician doesn't care for the rules or arrangements which the artist has established, he should pass on the job. If he takes the job, he should take it on the terms in which it was offered.

If the musician has been with an artist awhile and feels that he deserves a raise, he should speak with the band leader or artist directly, depending upon the situation, and discuss it in an orderly fashion. If the raise is not forthcoming in what the musician considers to be a reasonable period of time, then the musician should consider seeking another job with someone else. He should not start grumbling and complaining around the other musicians, most of whom probably feel some sense of loyalty to their employer, and are likely to mention that the musician is generating bad will among the troupe.

But the traveling musician does have rights. He has the right to be paid fairly and the right to be respected for his work and treated accordingly. If the artist is a jerk, and some are, then the unappreciated musician may foment a rebellion among the other musicians. While I am not advocating this line of action, I'm not saying not to do it either. But be aware that if you give someone an ultimatum, and they have no choice but to accept it, you must be prepared for the consequences later. And never, ever, threaten anybody with anything unless you're prepared to immediately make good on your threat.

In any case, if the artist spreads the word that you are a troublemaker, other artists will most likely not bother to find out the facts. They will decide not to hire the musician with such a reputation, regardless of whether the reputation is deserved.

When a musician is hired to play on the road, he is not being hired as a career adviser, and should not, unless asked, tell the artist how things "ought to be run around here." The artist already has a manager. On the other hand, if there is something which a musician sees which could be improved upon, it should be mentioned quietly at the right time to the right person.

Ideally, a sincere mutual respect exists between the artist and the band members. The players are well paid, are well treated, like each other and the artist, and, except for periods of extensive travel, enjoy the job. At the same time, the artist pays the money and is the boss. He cannot permit himself to have his life determined by the whims, moods, or demands of his band.

Finally, the successful road or studio musician who has survived and prospered in Nashville has learned to treat his work as a business. While most young musicians are swayed initially by the excitement of the road, things change when you get to Nashville. There is simply too much competition for work, and the musician who has been up all night raising hell will be unable to keep up with someone who is serious about what he's doing. The saying "Show up straight and don't be late" has never been more applicable to the professional musician.

The life of the professional musician is often subject to times of feast and famine. When things are going well and there is an abundance of work, the serious musician is likely to resent having any time off, and wonders, for example, why he isn't working in the studio during an open period. When this happens, the musician is likely to spend time worrying about the work that he doesn't have, when he should be concentrating on what's at hand. Also, the musician who works constantly is likely to lack the time for reflection necessary to really examine his music, and may become stagnant.

The rewards of playing on the road and hearing your instrument coming in at just the right moment in front of

an audience of ten thousand people is very rewarding to
the road musician. Driving down the street and hearing
your licks blasting out over the radio is an incredible
experience as well, and for the musician who views his
work as an art, being able to take part in the creation of
something significant, and being paid for it, are the
greatest rewards of all.

The Musicians' Union

The American Federation of Musicians was originally
founded in 1896, and according to its bylaws:

> The object of the American Federation of Musicians
> of the United States and Canada shall be to unite all
> professional musicians without discrimination, re-
> gardless of race, creed, sex, or national origin,
> through Local Unions into one grand organization
> for the purpose of:
>
> 1. Elevating and bettering the economic status, so-
> cial position, and general welfare of its members;
>
> 2. Negotiating collective bargaining agreements with
> employers on behalf of its members;
>
> 3. Providing assistance in contract administration
> and enforcement for the protection of its members;
>
> 4. Resolving grievances, disputes, and controversies
> among Locals, members, and employers;
>
> 5. Encouraging and training Local officers in repre-
> senting their members;
>
> 6. Advocating the interests of members and Local
> Unions to the public and governments; and encour-
> aging, promoting, supporting, and developing au-
> diences for the preservation, enjoyment, and
> appreciation of performances by professional
> musicians.

One of the primary functions of the union, both in

Nashville and in New York, is negotiating and bargaining with employers on behalf of members. For example, locally, the AF of M has negotiated the Nashville Symphony Agreement for the more than seventy-five classical musicians in the Nashville Symphony and has represented musicians dealing with Opryland, as well as bargained collectively for the musicians performing on the Grand Ole Opry, one of the longest-running radio shows in history. Other national agreements affecting membership in locals throughout the United States and Canada, such as the Phonograph Labor Agreement, Documentary and Industrial Films Agreement, Basic Theatrical Motion Picture Agreement, and other television and motion picture agreements, have all protected the musicians working in those fields and have standardized labor practices.

In addition, the AF of M hosts national conferences for the International Conference of Symphony and Opera Musicians, the Regional Orchestra Players' Association, and the Recording Musicians Association. The *International Musician*, a national publication, is sent to members, as well as local newsletters.

The musician's union also provides low-cost instrument insurance, access to group health insurance, through the Nashville local, as well as various trust, pension, and emergency relief funds and plans.

For the average recording-studio musician, the union has served to protect his interests in a number of practical ways. For example, a musician plays on a much-watched national television show originating in Nashville. The job of musician on this show is one many musicians would like to have. In fact, some musicians might be willing to work the job for less money just to have steady work. Another musician might be willing to work the show for nothing, just to get national exposure.

The union, through its influence and negotiations,

makes certain that the employer can't get away with conducting a bidding war in which the lowest-paid musician is hired. In other words, scale on a particular engagement is what any musician should and will receive. Some musicians charge more than scale. A studio picker who is in high demand can charge two or three times union scale for his services. There is no limit. He just can't work a union session for less than scale.

Of practical interest to the musician is the union's retirement fund, which is paid into by the musicians and given back to them incrementally. For many musicians, in fact for nearly everyone in the music business, there is no retirement plan of any kind. When the work stops, you are out of money. This is true for most talent agents, producers, managers, and other executives in all branches. While some record labels may have retirement plans, very few people survive in one job at one place long enough to reap any substantial benefit. The retirement plan offered by the union offsets this at least to some degree for the professional musician.

Being a professional musician in Nashville can be a very rewarding career, and while more and more musicians continue to flock to Nashville, the number of outlets for their services grow as well. Nashville is truly Music City, U.S.A., and most of the successful musicians who live here find the vibes to be great, and the interaction with other artists and musicians stimulating.

8

Publishing and Songwriting

While most people agree that the good songwriter generally possesses some innate talent that emerges early in life, almost all believe that it is an ability which can be expanded upon and developed more successfully through practice. So is the songwriter born or made? Both. But the born songwriter can become better by working at his craft.

There are, in fact, very few songwriters who wrote hits right from the beginning. Learning to write successfully is an art which is developed over time. Looking back at their first efforts, many will tell you that they weren't very good. Yet somebody, somewhere, saw something in these young writers and offered them some encouragement. This is one of the important reasons for writing with other writers, especially writers who are already established. You not only receive encouragement, but you also get instruction and an honest evaluation of your work.

Under ideal circumstances, it is the passion of the songwriter which animates his work, the desire to be a part of the creative process. While a number of present-day songwriters are excellent musicians, some with technical training, other successful songwriters do not read music, can't sing, and can hardly play an instrument, and yet they are great at coming up with lyrics and melody. Much of country music is not that complex, and a significant part of it is written around three basic chords.

The Function of the Songwriter

The primary function of the songwriter is to write commercial songs which are recorded by successful artists, become hit songs, and make money. The songwriter who brags about having written over a hundred songs is not in the same league as the writer who has written one hit song and had it recorded, played on the radio, and sold.

When Do You Quit?

Becoming a successful songwriter takes time, in developing skills as well as in networking, creating business relationships, and getting a reputation established. A period of five years is not uncommon. Also, songs sometimes sit around in catalogues undiscovered and unrecorded for years.

Many people give up too soon, believing that they can just speed-write some hit songs and everybody will come running. When this doesn't happen within six months, they give up and return home, feeling that they have honestly given it their best shot. Perhaps they have.

Becoming successful as a songwriter is well worth the time and effort. No greater thrill exists than to have *your* words and music interpreted by a producer, studio musicians, and a popular artist and played over the radio nationwide.

If you have what it takes to make it as a songwriter,

you will hold this vision in your mind's eye, imagine yourself accepting awards at the ASCAP or BMI dinner, and keep writing. Ultimately, the harder you are willing to work, the luckier you are likely to be. If songwriting is really your passion, and if you have talent and can overcome the trials you will encounter, you will probably have a rewarding career.

The Bluebird

While there are many great places in Nashville where songwriters congregate to play their songs, meet new people, and generally network, the Bluebird is unique in Nashville in its position as the premier accoustic listening room. This small but intimate nightclub is a favorite haunt of songwriters and musicians. The neophyte musician will find an open mike night at the Bluebird on Mondays, and songwriters and singers can sign up at five-thirty to play on the show that night. The show runs from six o'clock until nine. Usually, however, only about half of those who sign up are allowed to play that night due to the constraints of time. Those who do not get a chance to perform play the following Monday night, so nobody really has to wait three months to play, as is commonly thought. Technically, one could play a couple of songs at the Bluebird every other Monday.

There are quarterly auditions for those wanting to play a full show. More than a hundred people show up for these auditions. Between thirty and thirty-five of them will be rejected by the judges. Four of those who make it will be placed with five who have played before on the weekly Sunday night writers' show.

About six hundred people appear on a continuing rotation at the Bluebird, which means that over the course of fifty Sundays, each of these writers is only going to be playing once a year. One of the Bluebird's most successful features is known as "In the Round," and features several well-known songwriters sitting around in a circle, taking turns playing their songs.

But there are other writers' nights throughout Nashville, and the aspiring songwriter should seek to play those as well. There are about twenty open mike shows in Nashville on any given night, enough so that someone could play an open mike night every single night of the week. Record company execs do attend writers' nights, though not always, and usually for the express purpose of checking out a particular writer or singer whose name has come to their attention. On the other hand, new and hungry managers, publishers, and record company execs come because they are constantly seeking new talent and want to make a name for themselves.

The Buzz

Nashville is a buzz town, and in order for a writer to get a buzz or burst of interest and enthusiasm going about his work, it's important to generate action on as many fronts at the same time as possible. Ideally, word should be spreading from one person to another. This applies equally to songwriters as well as artists. Playing different writers' nights, attending local functions, and tapping into the energy stream in Nashville is essential to any writer's success.

But the buzz is a fleeting thing, and if not sufficiently nourished, it will die. When the interest which seemed to be so high begins to wane, the writer or artist may feel a sense of desperation. His alarm is justified, especially if a certain career level hasn't been reached when things begin to slow down.

NSAI

The Nashville Songwriters Association International, better known as NSAI, is a not-for-profit trade association for songwriters established in Nashville in 1967, by songwriters seeking to help each other and to encourage and assist new writers. As such, NSAI is probably the single most important, as well as the first, contact for an aspiring songwriter to make in Music City. NSAI publishes several highly informative brochures for prospective writers. It also provides many helpful services for members: regional workshops for those who live outside Nashville, a song evaluation service, a toll-free hotline, a discount bookstore, a Nashville songwriters' workshop, use of Nashville office facilities, a guide to NSAI services, and the *Leadsheet,* a quarterly newsletter. There is also a counseling service which helps songwriters set goals and establish priorities.

The annual Spring Symposium, for example, is a four day conference which covers everything any songwriter would need to know about the process and the business of songwriting and music publishing. Topics addressed include how to set goals, create a commercial song, handle demos, deal with contracts, find a cowriter, and everything else imaginable, from evaluations of your existing songs to question-and-answer sessions with successful and established songwriters. Hotel and airline discounts are available.

NSAI provides hard-hitting information and direction to songwriters and pulls no punches about what it takes to make it as a successful songwriter. It is only by understanding and facing the many obstacles which exist in the real world that serious progress can be made for the aspiring songwriter. As an example, I quote from a brochure entitled "Songwriting…How Serious Are You?"

Ten Tips for Serious Songwriters

1. Get serious. The fact that you have written one or two songs does not mean that you are a songwriter, only that you think that you want to become one.

2. Get prepared to experience a long and challenging road. The process of learning how to write commercial songs usually takes years of hard work.

3. Never pay a publisher or a talent scout. Always ask a lot of questions and check the reputability of anyone or any company before you do business with them. Reputable contracts with reputable companies are priceless.

4. If you do not live near one of the major music centers (NY, LA, or Nashville), get involved with your local or regional music community to meet potential cowriters and establish a network of support for your talent.

5. Do not contact famous recording artists, major publishers, or record labels until you know how to do it correctly. Join NSAI and develop your songwriting skills, contacts, and knowledge about the business, and you will learn the procedures.

6. Elaborate demo tapes are expensive and not necessary. A simple guitar/piano vocal demo is fine, provided the material is presented in a professional manner.

7. Get permission from a specific person at a company before you send your material. "Unsolicited" means that no one has requested your package. It will be returned unopened and marked "unsolicited" if you have not received permission to send it.

8. Organize an effective recordkeeping method to document who you called, what song you submitted, and when you mailed it. Remember to be polite and professional with your follow-up.

9. Don't become defensive when you ask someone for

an opinion. By remaining open to constructive criticism on your material, you will further your knowledge about the craft of songwriting.

10. In order to become a great songwriter, you must write, write, write...and then...write some more.

NSAI exists to help and serve songwriters and potential songwriters, so if you are thinking of becoming a songwriter, this is the best place to start. This is true even if you haven't decided whether to move to Nashville. At the time of this writing, there are three levels of membership: the Associate membership (seventy dollars), for songwriters who are unpublished; the Active membership (seventy dollars) for songwriters who have at least one song with a music publisher; and the Student membership (thirty-five dollars), for full-time college or high school students.

Information on membership and other services may be obtained by contacting NSAI directly at the following address:

NSAI
15 Music Square West
Nashville, Tennessee 37203
Phone: 615-256-3354

In Nashville there are probably more successful songwriters per square mile than anywhere else in the world. Competition is high, but so is the energy, the spirit of companionship, and the thrill of creating music. If you have made the decision to pursue songwriting as your life's work and are willing to endure the learning process, you will, if successful, be rewarded with an incredible degree of personal satisfaction, financial independence, and freedom.

Music Publishing

The music publishing company is in business to make money. It accomplishes this objective by acquiring ownership of songs and using its power and influence to get the songs it owns recorded, and then collecting royalties from the sales and use of its materials. The publishing company which has hundreds of songs which nobody wants to record is not in as good a position as the one which has even a few songs successfully recorded. The songs which a music publisher owns is known as its catalogue. The songs which it has in its catalogue are what determines a publishing company's value. Companies whose catalogues contain large numbers of income-producing songs are in the best position of all.

Songs are usually acquired by a music publisher in one of several ways. A publisher may buy an existing company, taking over the songs it owns and adding them to its catalogue. The publisher may also selectively buy an individual song or songs from another publisher, or the publisher may hire writers to write for it. The writer who has a "publishing deal" with a music publisher is known as a staff writer.

Copyrights

A copyright for a song is much like the title to a car. It proves that you are the owner. If you want to sell or rent your car to somebody, you need to be able to prove that you own the car. It's the same for songs. The registered copyright serves as the title to the song.

So how does one get a song copyrighted? Technically, as soon as your song is written it is protected under copyright laws. This protection without registration exists basically in theory only. People do steal songs, both intentionally and unintentionally. In order to be safe, your copyright needs to be registered.

Having a song registered with the Copyright Office will not stop someone from stealing your song and reworking the lyrics, or taking your idea and rewriting it. What a copyright registration can do is establish a date of creation, which will be helpful if it should become necessary to protect your interests in court later on.

Most music publishing companies have copyright forms on hand and may give you one or more. Generally speaking, however, copyright forms are obtained by written request from the Copyright Office, at the following address:

Copyright Office
Library of Congress
Washington, DC 20559

or by phoning 202-707-9100.

When you have received your forms in the mail, you are required to submit one copy of your unpublished song and a twenty-dollar registration fee. Your song can be copyrighted merely as a lyric sheet without music.

Setting Up a Publishing Company

Many people want to be in the music publishing business. It can be, however, an expensive proposition. In the first place, for a publishing company to operate, it must have songs to sell. Unless these songs have come to a publisher through the purchase of an already existing catalogue, the publisher will have to hire writers. The expenses faced by the publisher are both immediate and continuing. A publisher usually advances several writers a weekly draw, has a place of business, phone, electricity, demo costs, a receptionist, a song plugger, and other employees. Until a publisher has had many songs recorded successfully, with money coming in regularly, it is in a potentially long-term position of negative cash flow.

According to several successful publishers and performance rights representatives, the rule is, Don't expect to see a profit for at least five years. If you understand this rule, you will be less likely to suffer financial and psychological damage when things don't move as rapidly as expected. Success may come in less time, or it may not come at all, but five years is a reasonable estimate.

How It Works

If you, as a songwriter, get a deal writing for a publisher, then the publisher is advancing you a weekly or monthly amount against future royalties. The publisher owns the song. The song is divided into two parts, the writer's half and the publisher's half. There are two types of royalties, performance and mechanical. When a record is sold, the publisher and writer are paid what are known as mechanical royalties. When a song is played, the publisher and writer are paid performance royalties. The mechanical royalties are paid by the record company, and the performance royalties are paid by the performance rights organizations.

As a writer, you are expected to be writing and not goofing off. Most music publishers have writing rooms, usually with a small piano or some guitars, and writers are expected to be working on a regular basis. How an individual songwriter gets his job done, where, and how much time he spends doing it, are not as important to the publisher as is the fact that good songs are being written regularly. In a songwriting arrangement with a publisher, a writer is usually expected to produce a certain number of songs monthly. This number varies according to writer and publisher.

How a songwriter comes up with new songs and material and involves himself in the creative process varies from person to person. Some writers are disciplined and write at regularly scheduled times, whether they feel like it or not. By doing so, they accustom themselves to the process of writing. Often what is produced under such forced circumstances is not very good.

But some writers feel that eventually they will be able to write well on command. In fact, in a cowriting situation, a writer may write with several different writers during the course of a week or month, and more or less have to write on command. These cowriting sessions are scheduled at a specific time on a specific date, often two or three times in one day. One writer may be better at lyrics, another's forte may be ideas, and a third may be great at melody.

When a writer schedules a cowriting session two weeks or longer in the future, he has no idea whether or not he will feel like writing when that time actually arrives. For this reason, it is good for a writer to develop the ability to write when necessary.

Other writers consider one of the benefits of songwriting the freedom to write when the spirit moves them. They work regularly on a daily basis but allow themselves the freedom to enjoy a particularly beautiful day or take time off. Some writers work only haphazardly in the summer but work every day in winter. It all depends on the individual, and yet it must always be kept in mind that freedom and responsibility go hand in hand. One thing is certain. The writer who wants to be successful needs to take his work seriously, for if he fails to make a living at his chosen profession, he's liable to end up working somewhere else with very little personal freedom.

The Writer's Contract With the Publisher

Here, as with all contracts in the music business, the term, or length, of the contract itself is open to negotiation. Many feel that any writer, especially a new one, needs a contract for more than a year. A year with two renewable options on the part of the publisher seems to be acceptable under most circumstances. Any contract with options on the part of the other party is essentially a contract for the duration of the options. In other words, If a publisher is signing you up as a writer for a year with two one-year extensions at its option, what it really means is that if the publisher isn't satisfied with your work, it can drop you after the first year. If it wants to continue the agreement under the same terms, the publisher can do so for up to another two years.

As mentioned in chapter 2, it is always prudent to have a competent attorney review and explain any contract with a publisher, or anyone else, before you sign it, no matter how smart you think you are. Overlooking what seems like one minor point can tie you up for several years.

Why would a writer and a publisher part company? The publisher might not feel that the writer is producing enough good songs on a regular basis, or there may be a personality clash between the writer and others who work for the publisher. I've been told by several successful writers that the number of songs a writer has recorded is often proportional to the degree which the writer fawns over the executives at his publishing company. Nashville is power crazy, and people at the top, or on the way up, in all branches of the music business like having power and enjoy wielding it.

Usually when a writer leaves a publisher at the end of the contract, he has received a better offer or feels that the publisher hasn't done a good enough job getting his songs placed. Writers, like artists, want to be the first priority at whatever music publisher they write for. When a writer and publisher part company, the songs the writer wrote while with that publisher remain the property of the publisher.

The Larger Versus the Smaller Publisher

"If I were a writer, I would prefer to be at a smaller publisher. I just feel like you get lost in the shuffle at a larger company." This statement was made to me by an official at one of the performing rights organizations and reflects the attitude of many writers. It is obviously not an opinion shared by the larger publishing companies.

Most songwriters would prefer to own all of their own songs and not have to deal with a publisher at all. A few are able to do so. Most writers use the publisher as a bank, from whom they receive money as an advance against future royalties. Often, large publishers have more money and are willing or able to give a writer a bigger weekly or monthly advance.

The Song Plugger

The song plugger is the person at the publishing company who submits songs to different record labels, producers, and artists, for the purpose of persuading specific artists to record the song or songs his company owns. The song plugger is likely the most important person at any music publisher. In fact, it could accurately be said, for the new songwriter, at least, that any music publisher is only as good as its song pluggers. It doesn't matter how many potential hit songs a publisher lists in the catalogue. No song is a hit until it has been recorded and has sold enough copies to justify the term. For this reason, getting songs recorded is a matter of top priority.

The song plugger's success will depend on a number of factors. His personal contacts are a top priority. As in every other branch of the music business, success in this field is largely based on relationships. The song plugger must create, establish, and sustain relationships which will put him on the inside track. He must find out which artists are recording and when. He must know their labels and producers. He must get his songs to the right people by any means possible.

Furthermore, the song plugger must be sharp enough to match a specific song with a particular artist, and get it right the first time. He must learn what works and how to close a deal, he must be able to do it frequently, and he must make it stick. It's nice to have an artist or producer place a song on hold, but doing so doesn't make the writer or the publisher any money. The song must be recorded.

Often the song plugger is spoken of disparagingly by songwriters. I have heard successful songwriters say that getting their songs recorded has in each case been the result of their own efforts, and not because a plugger pitched their material. The smart writer will get out and make the necessary contacts with labels, artists, and producers himself and won't wait around on the chance that a song plugger will pitch his songs diligently. In fact, at most large publishers, the writers who have already established themselves will receive the most attention.

The hungry and talented writer shouldn't agree to wait his turn. As in so many aspects of this business, he may very well have create his own opportunity. While there is a fraternity of songwriters in Nashville, songwriting is a very competitive business. People are fighting to get to the top, and others are fighting just as hard to stay there. The songwriter is advised to take the initiative.

The song plugger, like everyone else, is out to develop a name for himself and to make as much money as possible. His job is difficult, in that there are dozens of other competitors in the same field, each attempting to get songs recorded by specific artists. The ideal situation is for the song plugger to get a single release cut by a famous artist on every song he pitches, but this is not likely to happen in the real world.

Song pluggers are usually paid a base salary and a percentage or bonus of some sort based upon job performance, that is, the number of cuts they get for the publisher. From my conversations with various songwriters, it seems that of all the jobs most needed in the music business, the job of the song plugger probably comes first and has the greatest future in the next five years. The independent song plugger can represent individual songwriters and publishers on a per-song basis, without having to try to push songs which are unlikely to make it.

Do Songs Get Stolen?

Frequently one hears or reads in the paper that somebody is suing somebody else for having stolen a song, recorded it, and claimed it as his own. This occurrence is somewhat like a plane crash. When it happens, you hear about it, but in terms of the number of songs which are actually written and recorded, the number is very small. In most cases, when two songs sound similar, either musically or lyrically, it's usually a matter of coincidence. At the same time, if you have come up with what you think is a killer idea for a song, chances are that someone else has also thought of the same thing or soon will.

Be that as it may, sometimes songs are intentionally stolen. Not everyone is honorable, and a good writer can take the punch line or idea from a song and alter it just enough that it will pass for a different song. This happens more than anyone in Nashville cares to publicly acknowledge.

In any case, the best thing a songwriter can do is to copyright his material before he tries to get a record or publishing deal. If you hear a song which you know that you wrote on the radio, you will have to defend your interests, which means not only that you will have to hire an attorney, but that you will waste time and money which you may not have. Furthermore, after a song is out and doing well, there is an automatic tendency to think that the complaining writer is merely a troublesome and obnoxious whiner, regardless of the facts. The burden of proof will be on you if you decide to initiate legal action.

The best protection for your songs is to cover yourself every step of the way. First of all, copyright your material by registering it with the Copyright Office as discussed above. Having done this, keep a record of whom you play your song for, when, and under what circumstances, and where you leave tape copies and lyric sheets. Don't be randomly sending your songs to addresses in magazines and to people whom you don't know. A hit song is an incredibly valuable piece of property; treat it accordingly.

At the same time, in order to have your songs recorded or to get a staff writing job at a publishing company, you have to play your material for a number of people. If you start acting weird about it, as though you are guarding some priceless treasures, you're going to irritate people who could help you, and at worst make them think you're crazy. It's a delicate balance, but if you have any sense, you'll know what to do at the appropriate time.

Unsolicited Material

While this subject was touched upon briefly earlier in this chapter, I would like to address it in greater detail now.

Many writers have encountered the problem of publishing companies not accepting their material and marking it "return to sender" or "unsolicited" without even having listening to it first to determine whether they would be interested. After all, how hard can it be to listen to a few songs? This can understandably be very discouraging to the prospective songwriter who has labored to write and demo a song or songs.

"Aren't these people in business to get hit songs for their catalogue? How can they turn down material without even listening to see what it is? They could theoretically be passing on some of the greatest commercial songs and songwriters of all time, and without even listening first."

This is a legitimate complaint for many aspiring songwriters, and the reasons for their rejections may seem incomprehensible at first but will become clearer as we examine them.

With the convenient availability of inexpensive high-tech recording equipment, it is much easier now than ever before to demo and duplicate songs in large quantities. This easy production of cassette tapes and the increased popularity of country music have combined to create a huge output of unsolicited incoming material. The same person might mail tapes to several record companies, music publishers, performance rights organizations, management companies, agencies, artists, and even recording studios. Often these packages contain handwritten letters which are difficult to read, requests for response, instructions for returning tapes by mail, illegible handwritten lyric sheets, and so on. To deal with the incredible amount of unsolicited material, a major music publishing company would most likely have to hire not one but several people to filter through these tapes all day, every day.

Also, many publishers say that the time involved in dealing with a large volume of unsolicited material isn't really worth the trouble. While music publishers are in business to find hit songs and get them recorded, experience has shown that most of the material coming through the mail isn't, as a rule, that good. In other words, while there might be some truly great unsolicited material received through the mail, the publisher finds it more effective to work with what he already has.

Another reason both publishing and record companies are adverse to accepting unsolicited material is because the writer or artist could accuse them of stealing his songs. Such things, while rare, do happen, and for the record company, the likelihood of reward doesn't equal the risk involved.

No One Owes You a Response

If you send anyone in the music business in Nashville a cassette tape, record, CD, or anything else to listen to, don't ask for it back. In the first place, if somebody takes the time to listen to it, they have already done you a favor. It is inconsiderate to expect someone to take the time out of his busy schedule to listen to a song or songs and then go to the trouble to send the tape back to you. "But," you say, "I included a stamped self-addressed envelope." So what? Asking for or expecting someone to return a tape is like saying that your tape is more important and valuable than his time, which it probably isn't.

It is difficult to be heard or have your music listened to if you are mailing your tape to an address and not to someone in particular. There are several music business directories which list the addresses of the record companies, publishers, managers, and agencies, as well as the names of certain key personnel. If your submission is addressed to someone specifically, it has a much better chance of going beyond the "return to sender" box, but it is still not likely to reach its desired destination. The best way get your tape heard is to talk to somebody specific. This is another value of networking. "So-and-so told me to call you" is much better than calling somebody you don't know and who doesn't know you or hasn't heard of you.

If you can get somebody on the phone, chances are you can at least get your music heard if you approach that person in the right way. Publishers are actively seeking hit songs, but you have to get your foot in the door to be heard. This is not as difficult in publishing as it is with trying to get heard by a record company.

Again, if you are in Nashville, you can call in person. Sometimes the best thing is to establish contact with the person most likely to stop your tape before it gets to the individual you want to hear it, that is, the receptionist or secretary. This is potentially a difficult task, since Nashville music business receptionists are sometimes abrupt and chilly. It's their job to see that volumes of garbage don't get through, not to be mean, but so that the people who employ them can get their work done.

In many cases, however, the situation is worsened when the receptionist or secretary realizes the power he or she holds, and adds a strong dose of ego to the mix. They love being in a position to say no to as many people as possible. Some of these people are really all right once you get to know them, and can be persuaded on occasion to not only permit something to get beyond them but actually assist with the process.

For this to happen, you need to develop a friendly and conversational relationship with this person, at least over the phone. This is also difficult, because the secretary or assistant is most likely very busy answering the phone, taking messages, and transferring calls. The best thing for you to do is be in Nashville, where it is possible to network with others and accomplish much more than you can long distance, over the phone.

The main thing is to talk to an individual in a position of authority, if possible. If you can talk to someone and get him to remember who you are, without becoming a nuisance, chances are that you can persuade him or her to see that so-and-so gets your tape. It's a delicate balance, being pushy enough to get things done but not so pushy as to be obnoxious. There is no one correct way to do this. There are literally dozens of publishing companies in Nashville, so if you don't do well at first, you will have plenty of opportunity to work on developing successful phone skills.

How Many Songs on a Tape?

So how many songs do you put on a tape that you want to send to, or play for, somebody? Some record people feel that if you have one really great song you wish to pitch, it will be diluted if other, lesser songs are also put on the tape. When I asked one producer this question, he replied by asking, "How many great songs do you have?" Others told me that no more than three songs should ever be put on a tape. The correct answer is really the personal preference of whomever you intend to play the tape for or send it to. So ask. Otherwise, use your own discretion. Only submit your best material on the tape.

The old saying "You never have a second chance to make a first impression" is particularly true as far as submitting material is concerned. If you are able to present your material or have someone listen to it, the song needs to be really good. If it isn't, no matter how hard it was to get through to somebody the first time, it will be much harder the second time if what you initially played didn't catch his ear.

If you aren't prepared to submit something quite yet, then hold off until you are. If so-and-so is a friend of yours and can get an important person at a record label to give you a listen, wait until you are ready with your best music. Chances are that you feel you have at least ten really great songs. If this is the case, avoid the temptation to load the tape down with more than anyone wants to hear, or for that matter will even listen to.

Again, your purpose in playing or sending a tape should be kept in mind as well. If you are submitting a tape to a record company for consideration as an artist, your objectives will be a bit different than they would be if you are submitting a tape to a publisher in order to provide a sample of your writing skills.

"Some people send their material on the best quality tape available, just to be sure that they sound as absolutely bad as possible." Someone made this observation casually a few years ago, and I found it amusing. The best tapes to record on are those appropriate to the length of the material included. If you are sending two songs, put them on a short medium-quality tape. There is no reason to send two songs on a ninety-minute, highest-quality tape. Sending a couple of songs on a maximum-quality brand-name tape just makes it more likely that your material will be recorded over when someone is looking around for a high-quality tape on the spur of the moment. Short, medium-quality no-name tapes are the best.

Label the tape. While it's a good idea to label the cassette tape cover both on the side and on the top, that is not enough. Always label the tape, on the tape. If space is limited and you cannot list the song titles, at least print your name and phone number with a note like "4 songs." The specific song titles can be included on the tape cover insert, which should also contain your name and phone number. You should place your address somewhere on the package, but your name and phone number are the most important items.

If the material you have submitted has been heard and deemed to be so incredible that you must be reached immediately, nobody is going to write you a letter. They will try to reach you by phone. Again, your phone number is the single most important item. I am harping on this because often people think somebody will go to the trouble of writing some lengthy critique. Nobody has time for that anymore. Always make everything as easy as possible for whomever you are trying to reach or persuade.

So, let's recap the minimum requirements for the aspiring songwriter. Live in Nashville, network, write, and don't give up. If you follow these simple instructions, and you have talent, the chances are that you will do well here in the Music City.

9

Performance Rights Organizations

According to the U.S. government, "A performing rights society is an association or corporation that licenses the public performance of nondramatic musical works on behalf of the copyright owners."

Many people have looked at a record label or album cover and seen, in addition to the song title, the writer's name, publishing information, and the letters BMI, ASCAP, or SESAC, and have wondered what those letters mean. They are abbreviations for the three performance rights organizations. BMI stands for Broadcast Music, Incorporated; ASCAP stands for the American Society of Composers, Authors and Publishers; and SESAC stands for the Society of European Stage Authors and Composers. That's fine, but what is a performance rights organization? The U.S. government, under various copyright laws, states that the owners and creators of original works have the right to license their works for performance purposes and to be paid for the licensing of their compositions.

In other words, the music you hear on the radio or on television or in a nightclub or restaurant was written by, and is owned by, somebody. When songs are used by a person or organization for the purpose of making a profit, the people who wrote and own these songs should be paid for their use. Permission to play these compositions must be obtained from the persons who own and wrote them.

Almost every business today uses music to increase sales. Restaurants, shopping malls, doctors' offices, banks, hospitals, and others play music to create a relaxed and pleasant atmosphere for the customer. Some of the other businesses or organizations subject to paying licensing fees for public performance of recorded music include amusement parks, airports, airlines, trade shows, conventions and expositions, cable, local and major television networks, radio stations, nightclubs, bars, private clubs, discos, dance halls, gyms, and more. All of these businesses are subject to the same copyright laws.

Theoretically, each music user should negotiate with and pay each songwriter and publisher directly for the right to use each piece of music every time it's played. While this is a good idea in theory, it is literally impossible to do so. In the first place, there is way too much music in the American marketplace, let alone the world, for any one person to keep up with it all. According to BMI, there are over seventy-five thousand places currently playing recorded music publicly in the United States alone. Since it would be impossible for any individual writer or music publisher to monitor when, if, and how many times a certain song was played, this function is accomplished by the performance rights organizations, which act on behalf of affiliated writers and publishers.

ASCAP, BMI, and SESAC negotiate with individual businesses on behalf of the songwriters and publishers and grant these businesses licenses to play songs from their respective catalogues. The function of a performance rights organization is actually threefold: It licenses music, collects licensing fees from the people playing it, and distributes royalties to its member writers and publishers.

We should next examine the difference between the various types of rights, since this can seem confusing. Basically, there are performance, mechanical, and synchronization rights. Performance rights generally apply to music which is played on television or on the radio. Mechanical rights generally apply to music which is sold, such as records, tapes, or CDs. Performance rights royalties are paid to the publishers and writers by the performance rights organizations, while mechanical rights are paid by the record company. Synchronization rights apply to music on film, that is, movie soundtracks.

For the Songwriter to be Paid

In order to be paid for public performance of songs, songwriters and publishers must be a member of a performance rights organization. This money is collected and then turned over to the writers and publishers. All songs, whether country, rock, pop, classical, jazz, blues, or any other form of music, are licensed by and through one of the performance rights organizations.

Tracking

It is truly impossible to know exactly what stations are playing what songs anywhere in the nation at any specific time. Since the publishers and writers are paid according to the total number of times their songs are played nationally, tracking the number of performances is therefore a primary concern, not only to the writer and publisher of recorded material but also to the performance rights organizations.

Each of the three organizations employs slightly different tracking techniques. SESAC uses "sophisticated computer technology"; BMI uses "an elaborate computer system which multiplies each performance listed by a factor which reflects the ratio of the stations logged to the number licensed." Nobody really knows what this means in everyday language, but there is a great deal of actual performance monitoring by all three of the performance rights organizations.

BMI, for example, solves the monitoring problem by sampling a different cross-section of stations each quarter. The stations monitored provide BMI with their play-lists, which are then put through an elaborate and complex computerized system which determines averages. BMI logs approximately 500,000 hours of commercial radio and more than 50,000 hours of noncommercial radio broadcasts such as college radio each year.

Television music such as theme, background, and feature music is logged through specific information provided by the stations on cue sheets for all network programming. Cable and syndicated shows are monitored the same way, and thus performance royalties are paid on all network, cable, and syndicated performances. In fact, BMI tracks over 6 million hours of television programming annually.

While performance rights organizations do pay royaties to songwriters and publishers based upon the performance of songs in places like hotel lounges, restaurants, bars, and other similar places, it would be too difficult to correctly monitor each place. Instead, it is generally assumed that the music played in such places is consistent with what is being played on the radio at any given time, and estimated accordingly. Needless to say, this is not absolutely accurate, but it seems to be acceptable to those involved in the process.

What If a Business Refuses to Pay?

Often a new business will open and the employees or owners will unknowingly turn on a tape or radio for background music, not realizing that the music being used must be paid for. "Hell, it's just the radio," the business owner says. Frequently he has no idea that he must pay for having the radio on in the background. When it is brought to his attention, he's truly shocked and thinks he is being shaken down by some thug, like the victim of a protection racket shakedown in a gangster movie. After the situation is explained and the shock wears off, most businesses sign up and factor the licensing fee into their operating expense budget. The cost is not that great for the individual business.

Other business owners and operators do not feel that they owe anyone anything. If a business is playing copyrighted music and refuses to pay any of the performing rights organizations, it is very likely that legal measures will be taken to bring the offender into compliance with the law. Since copyright infringement fees can be very expensive, it is much easier for a business to sign agreements with the performance rights organizations to begin with. The performance rights organizations exist to protect writers, composers, and publishers and are actively involved in signing up new businesses. They all have representatives in the field who are out looking for violators.

How Is the Money Collected?

When a business signs a licensing agreement with BMI, it is for an initial term of one year. The annual fee must be paid at the time the contract is signed. Most customers pay an annual fee to ASCAP as well. Payment of these fees entitles the licensee to play any song or songs in the respective catalogues as many times as desired. The fees vary according to the size and type of operation and are determined by the hierarchies at the respective performance rights organizations.

Where Does the Money Go?

BMI and ASCAP are both "non-profit-making" corporations. All of the money they collect, minus operating costs, is paid directly to writers and publishers in the form of royalties. Operating costs include clerical and administrative costs, salaries, legal expenses, and other expenses any business would encounter.

Why One Instead of Another?

The business seeking to use recorded music will need to negotiate agreements with both BMI, ASCAP, and in some cases the Society of European Stage Authors and Composers (SESAC). Any radio station, for example, or other business playing recorded music is certain to play music represented by BMI and ASCAP and must negotiate with both organizations for the right to play such music. It isn't a matter of choice.

The publisher or writer must decide which performance rights organization he should join. Ultimately, this is an individual decision and is based on a number of subjective factors. ASCAP, BMI, and SESAC all make certain claims as to why you should be with "us" instead of with "them." In fact, how you feel after meeting with the people at these places is probably the most important point to consider. Get to know someone at each place. Does the place have a warm, friendly vibe, or is it cold and sterile? Ask other writers who are affiliated at different performance rights organizations and see what they have to say.

If you make a wrong decision, you can always move to a different organization at the expiration of the contract. Most publishers have a separate company for each performance rights organization, so that if a writer is hired who is already affiliated with BMI, for example, the publisher can have him write for its BMI company. The same would be true for ASCAP and SESAC.

Jobs

Job opportunities at at these three performance rights organizations appear to be good, especially for women. At ASCAP, Marilyn Bergman became chair of the board in January 1995. Francis Preston heads BMI, and until her departure from SESAC in early 1995, Diane Petty was in charge of the Nashville office. A college degree in business administration, with a minor in music business, is a good start for anyone seeking employment at one of the performance rights organizations. Having a famous artist or writer for a father doesn't hurt either.

BMI

10 Music Square East
Nashville, TN 37203
Phone: 615-401-2000; 800-669-4264 for businesses
   with questions about music licensing.

ASCAP

ASCAP has a toll-free number, 800-952-7227, which is manned live between the hours of nine A.M. and eight P.M. Monday through Friday.

ASCAP
2 Music Square West
Nashville, TN 37203
615-742-5000

ASCAP
1 Lincoln Plaza
New York, NY 10023
212-621-6000

ASCAP
7920 Sunset Boulevard,
   Suite 300
Los Angeles, CA 90046
213-883-1000

ASCAP
PO Box 11171
Chicago, IL 90046
312-481-1194

ASCAP
8 Cork Street
London W1X 1PB
011-44-71-439-0909

ASCAP
1519 Ponce De Leon
   Avenue, Suite 505
Santurce, Puerto Rico
   00909
809-725-1688

SESAC

SESAC
55 Music Square East
Nashville, TN 37203
615-320-0055

SESAC
421 West 54th Street
New York, NY
   10019-4405
212-586-3450

If you call any one of the three performance rights organizations listed above and request information, you will receive enough written material to keep you busy for quite a while. Representatives from any of the three organizations are available to answer any further questions or to schedule a meeting with prospective members.

10

The Manager

There are so many people who think that by merely buying an act, they earn the right to call themselves managers. Nothing could be further from the truth. It's like the owner of a sports team deciding that he is qualified to coach the team just because he owns it. A real manager, as we will see, is someone who devotes his or her *full time* to the development of an artist's career.

Nor is management a job which can be subcontracted. Whenever some starstruck doctor, lawyer, or other full time professional from another field thinks he can buy his way into the music business, he is invariably taken for a fool, and usually for a great deal of money as well.

The doctor or lawyer spends literally years learning the basics of his trade, and years more attaining an intuitive proficiency. Management, too, is a skill and an art, developed over time and through experience. It isn't something which can be bought, any more than one can buy a medical degree or a law degree. It is an insult to every real manager to have some big shot use the term "manager" casually. People who work full-time in the music business as managers handle the careers and fortunes of the artists whom they represent, as well as the careers and fortunes of the dozens of support people and their families who depend on the artist's success for their own livelihood.

A Brief History of the Manager in Country Music

In the early days of country music, the term "manager," at least in Nashville, had little meaning. Most people who served in the capacity of what we now call managers, performed many of the same tasks as managers do today, only without being paid for it. They were generally agents who took care of details associated with getting a show booked, played, and paid. Many of those who became first-generation music business executives started out as traveling musicians and sidemen. Some of them began as entertainers themselves, but in time realized for one reason or another that they weren't going to make it as stars, and turned their talents in other directions. There were no business management schools dealing with the music business as there are now. Most persons who became managers evolved into managers as an outgrowth of other, usually music-related jobs. This is often still true today, despite the existence of several colleges featuring music business curriculums.

The Role of the Manager

Ideally, the manager should be involved in an artist's career from beginning to end. This means nursing an artist along until he is ready for the manager to secure a record deal. However, most managers become involved after the record deal has been made. The recording contract is the first important step in any country artist's career, and if an artist doesn't have one, it's the first priority of the manager to get one for his artist.

To do this, the manager must have an artist who is really committed and has a shot at the big time. The manager must be able to present the artist in the best possible light, and be prepared to be turned down often, frequently by the same people. He must face apathy and disappointment as well as negativity from the artist and yet still be able to keep going and accomplish his objectives.

Another part of the manager's job is to surround the artist with good, solid, team players, including an agency, publicist, financial adviser, and others who help him develop personal, career, and financial security. With the record deal in place, the next part of the plan involves the selection of a talent agency for the artist's personal appearances.

Selecting an Agency

The ideal situation for a manager is to have his own agency in-house, where either he or other persons in his employ can serve as the artist's agents. In this way, the manager is able to solidify his position with the act and to prevent raids on his talent from other agencies and managers. He controls the entire career. If the artist wants to dump his manager, it will be more difficult to do so if the manager also controls his income.

There are certain advantages to this arrangement for the artist as well. His manager has a vested interest in seeing that the artist is working. With the manager being responsible for the dates, the artist is guaranteed top priority, something he would be unlikely to get at an agency which has dozens of acts, and other priorities. This is especially important in the early make-or-break stages of an artist's career. There is also absolute accountability. Nobody can dodge the responsibility for not doing his job by hiding under the umbrella with a dozen or more other agents.

While the idea of an in-house agency is good in theory, it is seldom done in the real world for the simple reason that booking an artist is a full-time job in its own right, as is management. To hire a competent full-time agent is an expensive proposition and is not financially feasible with a new act who hasn't made any money.

Selecting an agency is of primary importance in any artist's career. While this selection is sometimes made by the artist, the choice of agencies almost always involves the manager. While there are many factors involved in the selection of an agency, one must discover whether the agency has an opening for the type of act the manager is shopping. In other words, if the act the manager has signed a hat act, or a cowboy-hatted clone, in the $5,000-per-night range, the manager would not want to take him to an agency where there are three or four other similar acts in the same price range. Instead, he would seek an agency where there is a need for an act like the one he manages. The same thing applies to vocal groups, female artists, duos, and so on. The key rule here, as elsewhere, is to find a hole and fill it.

Another factor is the time element. While an agency may be very good, well respected, and effective, the agency's extensive client list or high artist-to-agent ratio may make it impossible or undesirable for the agency to take on any additional artists. This might not be the case six months from now. With that in mind, the manager will probably begin a preliminary search as soon as a record deal has been signed. By the time an artist's first release appears, the agency decision should have already been made.

The wise manager will usually keep as much distance between the agency and his act as possible, for the simple reason that the agency, as the primary source of both the artist's and manager's income, represents the biggest potential threat to the manager. This means the manager will want his artist to sign with an agency which will respect that boundary and not attempt to contact the artist directly and work behind the manager's back.

Since, under this scenario, the act will have little personal contact with the agency, the manager needs to find an agency he can trust and and a "responsible agent" within that agency whom he trusts, and hopefully likes. First he will look at agencies in general, then at particular agencies, and then at specific individual agents within those agencies. The artist's responsible agent is the individual agent within the artist's agency who has day-to-day contact with the manager or artist. Any offers of employment from other agents within the office are submitted to the responsible agent, who takes them to the manager or artist for approval. He is the liaison between the artist or manager and the rest of the agency.

The artist's responsible agent needs to wake up in the morning thinking about where he is going to book his artist that day. The manager will often speak with the act's responsible agent first thing in the morning, again after lunch, and again at the close of the day. These conversations usually address particular problems or areas of concern with the artist's date sheet or itinerary. The schedule of an artist's dates is addressed on two main levels, time and money. The manager will want to know what the agent has scheduled for the short term, medium term, and long term.

The immediate problems are, of course, the most important. For example, two weeks from now the artist has a Friday concert, a Sunday festival, and a Monday private party scheduled. He cannot afford to sit in a hotel room on Saturday night, paying his band and not working. The agent needs to fill the open date. This is an immediate short-term problem which must be addressed now. If the date doesn't get filled, the manager will understandably blame the agent or agency. Since the agent will not be present to defend himself, he will end up as the whipping boy.

While the agent is addressing immediate problems, the manager will also expect him to work on problems falling within the next four to six months. Long-term scheduling beyond the next six months must be addressed by the manager and agent as well. The problems the manager is concerned with usually involve how much money the artist is making, and how often and where the artist will be playing. It is to the agent's and the manager's personal advantage to see that the artist works as much as possible. Obviously, the more the artist works, the more the agent and manager make. Beyond that, however, are the real and more pressing financial concerns of the artist's day-to-day life, such as mortgage, bus, insurance, band, staff, and other ongoing expenses.

Another, and perhaps the determining, factor in selecting an agency, all other considerations being equal, is whether an agency really wants to take on the responsibility of booking the act. The successful agency's leaders know that the future of their business depends on signing as many superstars as possible. Since nobody knows for certain who these acts are likely to be, agencies have a tendency to sign almost any new artist on a major label, figuring they can always let him go if he becomes a problem or doesn't make it. Hedging the bet in this way is easier than trying to steal a successful artist from another agency after he's already made it.

The manager must be able to see beneath the agency's desire to sign just about any new act coming down the path, and determine who really can and really wants to work with his new artist. This is not as easy as it might seem. The manager can automatically disregard anyone who doesn't seem interested and enthusiastic about representing his new act. Agents are salesmen by nature. That's what they do for a living. To succeed, they must be convincing. Any agent worth a damn can say to the manager, "We really believe that your act is going to be a star, and we want to work with him."

The manager must be able to figure out who is sincere, and who is merely hedging a bet.

Similar decisions are involved all the way down the line as the artist and manager select the publicist, accountant, road manager, and other members of the artist's team. Each of these players is important, but the agent is probably the most crucial player after the manager and record company are in place.

The Manager and the Music

How much input should the manager have musically in the artist's career? There is no specific formula here. Some managers like to be involved in everything from the selection of material and producers to the choice of single releases for radio. The more facets of an artist's career in which the manager can be involved or control, the more secure his position with the artist will be. If the manager has a musical background and is qualified to make recommendations, his opinions may be acceptable, or even desirable. Other managers who are not qualified to have an opinion musically seek to express one anyway, and can become a liability to the artist. Still other managers readily acknowledge that their forte is business, not music, and wisely keep out of an area in the artist's career with which they may be unfamiliar.

While record companies frequently make mistakes in

the choice of a single release, it's probably in the best interest of the manager, in the long run, to let the record company and the artist pick the singles, and to concentrate his efforts on getting those singles played on the radio.

The Manager and the Artist's Team

Ultimately, the ideal situation is for the manager to have an extended overview of the artist's career and to monitor, but not seek to control, the work of the other members of the artist's team. A manager who has to constantly ride the agent, publicist, road manager, and others is likely to be ineffective, if for no other reason than he has surrounded his artist with the wrong support people. An efficient manager would most likely know enough to avoid that error by lining up the right people for those jobs in the first place.

The job of the manager is to do everything possible to further his artist's career. Every afternoon the manager should plot the next day's activities on his artist's behalf. No two artists are the same, so it's necessary to set specific goals for each client a manager may represent. Following up on ongoing projects and starting new ones occupies a big part of the manager's day.

At some point in his artist's career, a manager will most likely have dealings with someone at every level of the record company. Labels in Nashville seem to have evolved to the point that a division of labor and responsibilities exists operationally within the structure of the record label. In other words, a record label has to have separate creative and administrative departments.

Both are highly important to an artist's career. The marketing, promoting, merchandising, packaging, and business end fall under the administrative department.

The creative side of the label is responsible for recording and making records, picking singles, and so on. In dealing with the record company on a day-to-day basis, the manager's job consists of communicating and coordinating with the artist, the label, and all of the label's various departments.

Working with the marketing and promotional wings of the record company and with the talent agency, the manager can arrange for his artist to do promotional tours in which he visits radio stations in person and performs in key cities. With this kind of teamwork, the artist's radio airplay, record sales, ticket sales, and career are hopefully advanced through the joint efforts of the artist, manager, agent, and record company. Between the time that an artist is signed to a record label and the time that a single and an album are recorded, manufactured and released, six months to a year or longer will have elapsed, so there is plenty of time to work out a specific plan of action between the manager and the various departments of the record company.

Hopefully, the manager has been able to plan a targeted radio attack on the artist's behalf in advance, with the record company, making certain that there are no internal scheduling or other unforeseen conflicts within the record label or with the label's other artists. On the other hand, it is impossible to know what another record label is planning. For example, record releases by major acts like Reba McEntire, Garth Brooks, or other heavy hitters can swamp a new act. You can at best be aware of what your own label is doing, but you can't always accurately predict what the other twenty or so major labels are going to do at any given time.

To what extent, if any, should an artist be involved in the management of his own career? Again, this depends primarily upon the artist. As the level of sophistication of country artists has increased, as well as their educational background, more of them have become students of the music business. If the input an artist offers is based on knowledge, awareness, and experience, and divorced from ego, most managers will welcome the help.

It's certainly easier to persuade an artist to do an important interview after a show if he understands the underlying reasons and the likely positive effects on his own career. The more an artist knows about how things work, the better his career is likely to be. If the artist is an egomaniac, an idiot, or a jerk, however, his input will be not only undesirable and annoying, but something which must be overcome and bypassed as well.

Several times a year, the manager should coordinate and conduct a meeting between all of the various players on the artist's team. This group would include representatives from the various supporting structures and would consist of the manager, responsible agent, publicist, road manager, accountant, someone from the record company, and so on. The purpose of the meeting should be to establish both short-term and long-term plans of action intended to advance the artist's career to the next level. This means examining the artist's present circumstances as they really exist and setting reasonable but specific goals to work toward in the future. For example, the artist's team could try to figure out in what period of time an artist could be moved from the opening slot on a major tour to the middle spot, and ultimately to the position of headliner.

What the Manager Seeks in an Artist

What a manager looks for in an artist varies from manager to manager. At least with a new, unestablished artist, the manager must decide whether the artist has any talent. Does he have star potential? Does he write his own material? Is he a good writer? Does he have a good voice? Is the artist charismatic? Is he unique?

The manager then determines whether the artist has any bad habits or any excess baggage in the form of prior agreements and committments. Is the artist crazy? Is he someone with whom the manager feels he can work? These are all important questions which a manager asks himself and frequently others in determining whether he wishes to represent a particular act. Assuming that the artist is talented, and that the manager wants to work with him, the most significant consideration should be what type of person the artist is. The average artist is only an artist three or four hours a day. The remainder of the time he is a human being. If the artist isn't a good human being, the manager is better off not getting involved at all. If an artist isn't a nice person, the chances are very high that he won't have a career anyway.

It is in the best interests of a manager to sign the artist to a lengthy management contract as soon as possible, that is, if he is interested and wants to work with the artist. It is just the opposite with an artist. It is in the artist's best interest to delay signing a management contract if there are several managers interested in signing him, so that he can get to know all of them and make a fairly educated decision. On the other hand, if the artist waits too long, potential managers will likely feel like they are being toyed with, lose interest in the artist altogether, and move on. In theory, at least, it is advisable for the artist to sign the shortest possible contract. At the same time, however, if there is no real commitment from the artist, there is little incentive for the manager to make a full-scale commitment. Developing an artist's career takes time. It is very seldom done in a year. If an artist is intuitive, as many are, his intuition and instincts may help in choosing a manager.

Most managers want to have an artist signed before they make even the first phone call on his behalf. I feel this way personally as a result of my own experiences. Other managers, and they are in a definite minority, are willing to wait for a management contract, pending the procurement of a record deal on the artist's behalf. They proceed on an oral agreement that if they are able to get the artist a record deal, they will expect a management contract signed at that time. Part of this initial agreement to agree is the understanding that the manager who is shopping the artist to various labels on a speculative basis will be doing so exclusively. This means that he won't have to worry about somebody else—another managerial candidate, the artist's boyfriend or girlfriend, or some other imbecile or idiot—interfering with his work.

If the manager who has a verbal agreement with the artist gets wind of anybody else shopping the artist behind his back, he should discuss the situation immediately with the artist and explain to him how things work. If the artist doesn't understand or disagrees, the manager should drop the artist at once. No matter how great that artist might be, it's better not to fool with him at all. If an artist is a problem at the very beginning of his career, it will only get worse on the other end.

If He Doesn't Make It, Let Him Go

If, after making the rounds, there is no interest from the labels, the manager may let the artist go. As one prominent manager expressed it, "This business moves too slow to be hard." With only twenty or so major labels, it doesn't take that long to knock on all the doors and make the rounds. You go in with a tape or have the artist sing live. If they like it, you do a showcase so that the record people can see the artist perform a real show. If nobody is interested, you might dismiss the artist or keep 5 percent of everything as insurance.

Managing an Artist Without a Contract

What about the well-established artist who is already making money and already has a record deal? This is a tough call and will have several different answers depending on the artist in question and on the personality, position, and power of the manager.

For example, let's say that I have a personal policy of not managing any act without a signed exclusive management agreement. I have maintained this policy for years, and it has served me well. Then one day, out of the clear blue sky, a top artist calls me and expresses an interest in having me manage him. We arrange a meeting and both decide that we would like to work together. There is one problem though. He refuses to sign any kind of management contract. It has nothing to do with me personally, he says, he just doesn't want to be tied down if things don't work out between us. Becoming his manager will mean a big jump in income for me, as well as an increase in prestige.

Do I stick to my guns and tell him that I can't work as his manager without a contract, knowing that I well may lose him? Or do I cave in and take him on without a contract?

This is not a yes-or-no question, and there are no right and wrong answers. If you take on a client for management without a contract, he might brag about it to other artists. As a result, the next thing you know, one or more of your other acts tell you they won't resign with you when their contracts expire. Suddenly your level of personal security and peace of mind has been greatly compromised. It's ultimately an individual decision based on a particular set of circumstances which exist at a specific time.

The Nature of the Management Contract

Most managers feel that an acceptable management fee is anywhere from 15 percent to 25 percent of an artist's gross income. While some managers charge less, and others more, fees within this range are generally appropriate. Anything in excess of 25 percent makes it likely that the manager could have a problem legally later on, if an artist wants to get out of the contract. The artist might successfully argue in court that the manager took advantage of the artist's inexperience by charging him an unduly high fee for management services. While the artist may have had ample opportunity to read the contract, and was aware of its contents and signed it anyway, the court may find the manager at fault. Court cases involving the music business are extremely unpredictable and often have illogical and unexpected results. It's best for the manager to stay within an acceptable range to start with and avoid the problem altogether.

Like lawyers, most managers charge their clients for incidental expenses such as phone calls, airfare, and hotel rooms. This has been a common practice on the West Coast for years and, while not yet universal in Nashville, is certainly a more common practice now than in the past.

Length of the Contract

One thing that will be noted when examining the careers of artists who have been at the top for a long period of time is that many of them have long-standing relationships with the members of their team. Alabama and Dale

Morris, Crystal Gayle and the William Morris Agency, Jim Halsey and Roy Clark, Ken Kragen and Kenny Rogers, Jack McFadden and Buck Owens—the list goes on and on. You establish a working relationship with the right people and keep it in place. Most artists who find long-term success concentrate on their careers rather than losing time, energy, and momentum making changes and lateral moves. An intelligent and talented artist with good solid relationships that work well will enjoy a successful career.

The term, that is, length, of the contract varies from manager to manager. Most of the managers to whom I spoke preferred a term of at least five years. Considering the competitive nature of the business and the time required to get an artist off the ground, the chances are low that a manager will be able to financially recoup his time and effort in less time than that.

Provisions

The management contract is usually a lengthy instrument of ten or more pages. While there are no universal specific or "standard" contracts, all will contain certain key elements, and some will contain optional provisions individually tailored to a specific artist or set of circumstances. Among the provisions to be found within the average management contract are the following:

1. Length of contract (average of one to five years)

2. Amount of percentage manager will receive as compensation for his services (average of 10 to 25 percent)

3. A generally vague and nonspecific outline of the manager's duties, such as:

   a. Manager agrees to render such advice, guidance, counsel, and other services as artist may reasonably require.

    b. Manager agrees to represent artist as negotiator, to fix the terms governing all manner of disposition, use, and employment of artist's talents and the products thereof.

    c. Manager agrees to supervise artist's professional employment, to consult with employers and prospective employers on artist's behalf.

    d. Manager agrees to engage, discharge, and/or direct theatrical agents, booking agents, etc.

4. Any advances to artist will be recoupable from any royalties paid to artist under agreement, such as record royalties, performance income, etc.

5. Cure provisions allowing either party to resolve contractual disputes without voiding the contract.

6. Exclusivity provisions benefiting the manager but not the artist. The artist may not have any other managers, but the manager may manage other artists.

7. A limited power of attorney is in many cases granted to the manager in order to expedite the execution of personal appearance contracts and other related contracts and agreements.

8. The establishment of a jurisdiction as a reference point in the event it should later become necessary to legally address a dispute between the parties.

9. The stipulation that the artist will pursue his career to the best of his abilities.

The above provisions of the average management contract have been abbreviated for clarity. The real contract will contain a great degree of intentionally obtuse and verbose language so that the attorneys for both parties can justify their high fees for what are often, but not always, merely glorified computer forms.

As mentioned earlier, prior to signing any management contract, or anything else, you, as the artist, are advised to secure an attorney for your own protection. Do not merely ask him to read it over and tell you whether the contract is acceptable. Go over it yourself and be sure that you understand every word and each provision. If there is some particular passage which is incomprehensible to you, don't move on until you understand it completely. It is much better to be ignorant now than stupid later. Use your lawyer's expertise. That's what you're paying him for.

If you are pressured to sign a management contract, or any other contract, take your time. Don't allow yourself to be intimidated. This is an important part of your career, one which can tie you up for years.

Problems Faced by Managers

The manager, like the agent is subject to the whims of the artist, his family, and a host of other often negative people and influences. The artist's career, and consequently his ego and emotions, are in a state of constant flux. The manager is often unfairly blamed for unfavorable and frequently unavoidable turns in an artist's career. Under such circumstances, the manager is often the target and focal point of the artist's resentment over everything wrong in the artist's life.

How Does One Get a Job as a Manager?

The ideal situation for the newcomer is to get a job as an intern with an established manager or management company. If you are in Nashville to pursue a career in the country music business, either as a future executive or entertainer, the chances are high that you are already familiar with a majority of the country artists and their record labels. A call to the artist's record label or to the

Country Music Association will get you the names, addresses, and phone numbers of any artist's manager, agency, and publicist. If there is an artist whose career you admire, call and make an appointment with his manager.

"But what if he won't talk to me? Or what if I can't get past his secretary?"

In Nashville, you still have a very good chance of getting just about anybody on the phone if you handle yourself right. You *will* find a way to get to the manager, whether on the phone, in a club or in the parking lot. When you do talk to him or her, have your story ready. Know who he is, what he has done with the specific artist or artists he represents. Let the manager know that you have done your homework and are prepared.

Ask him for an appointment; tell him you are a writer and are doing a book on managers. Whatever it takes to get through the door, do it. Don't frighten the guy by stalking him or acting crazy. If you approach him at a restaurant, he might tell you to call him at his office in a few days, just to get rid of you. While there is always the possibility that you will be turned down, chances are that if you are persistent, you'll at least get a meeting, and that's the first step. This applies equally to management candidates as well as artists seeking managers.

When you finally do get an appointment, if a job is what you want, ask for it. If you're told that his company isn't hiring right now, or given some other valid rejection, get past it.

Let the rejection apply to someone else and not to you. You came for a job. That's why you are here, and that's what you want. You want to be a manager, you believe that the person you are talking to is one of the best, if not the best, in the business, and you want to learn from him. Make him want to hire you. Make him feel that he should hire you. It's that simple. Be prepared to work for free if necessary, at a menial job at first, and be genuinely thankful for the opportunity.

What are some of the qualifications for successful artist management? The manager has usually displayed some aptitude for the job fairly early in his career. Often it starts in high school or college or in the service. An aspiring musician who isn't quite good enough to be in a local band, or is the brother of one of the musicians, or is the social chairman for his high school or college fraternity, begins by booking bands. He might find one particular band interesting and serve as agent, manager, and road manager to make some extra money.

Someone can come into the position of manager in any number of ways. Lee Greenwood's former longtime manager, Larry McFaden, started out as Lee's bass player. Musicians often end up as managers. Managers also frequently emerge from the positions of road manager, agent or any other number of other backgrounds.

One way to manage a successful act is to marry the artist. This usually gets rid of the competition fairly quickly. Brenda Lee's husband has been her manager for years. So have the husbands of Reba McEntire, Tammy Wynette, and others. The spouse who serves as manager is potentially in the best position of all, provided neither the manager nor the client has wandering eyes, or other parts.

All in all, while artist management is a complicated and difficult job, it calls upon its practitioner to develop and hone all of his skills to their sharpest point. Management is not some fringe aspect of the music business, and if you become a successful full-time manager, you will be right in the middle of everything. While there is much work, long hours, and disappointment, there are also many personal rewards and benefits. The opportunity exists to become very rich, to meet and associate with famous and interesting people, and to travel to interesting places. Ultimately, for the manager, there is no greater success and financial reward than seeing an artist whose career you have developed become an international superstar.

11

Talent Buyers and Promoters

If you want to make it in country music, you will be doing a lot of business with the talent buyers and promoters. They hire artists and put on shows. They also represent the artist's largest source of income in most cases.

While there are exceptions, in the case of certain private parties, like weddings, for example, talent buyers are generally in business to make money. If this is taken into account and kept in mind, the motives of the talent buyer will remain clear, and his actions, more or less predictable. In this chapter, we will examine the different types of talent buyers, their motives, how they operate, and how they are likely to act in certain circumstances.

Types of Clubs

Chances are that as a professional musician, your first real appearance will take place at a club. There are several different types of clubs, such as listening rooms, honky-tonks, supper clubs, dance clubs, discos, coffeehouses, oldies clubs, jazz rooms, urban, hip-hop, alternative, country, and more. While some of these distinctions and categories are important, the most significant consideration for the country artist is the size of the place. A club with an audience capacity of 1,500 or more is in a position to use big-name national acts in every category. Most club owners will showcase different types of acts if an opportunity exists to make money. A large club on an off night, with a major act passing through, often presents such an opportunity. Be that as it may, the distinctions between the various clubs are not important to the country artist or agent, except whether a country act is likely to find employment there.

The Listening Room

Just about every city across the nation has one or more listening rooms. These rooms almost always sell alcohol and are almost always small. Some believe they are doing an artist a big favor to permit him to play there. These clubs usually have a line of people waiting to get in and a waiting list for artists who wish to play there. The club owner charges admission and makes money at the bar and on food. The owners generally want the artist to work for nothing, or next to nothing they don't want to spend any money on advertising, and they want the record company, where one exists, to buy a certain number of drinks or tickets or to guarantee a minimum cash amount per person to the club.

At the same time, listening rooms serve a purpose. The atmosphere is almost always intimate, due to the small size of the room, and the sound is usually excellent. Most listening rooms are open to alternative music such as folk, reggae, and country, provided the country is pure, authentic, and has a certain snob appeal, regardless of how it sounds. Some want only accoustic music. For-

tunately, these are rare, at least as far as the mainstream
country act of today is concerned.

The Country Nightclub

The large honky-tonk or nightclub is a different matter
altogether, and the patrons are there for a number of
reasons, music being one of them but not necessarily the
most important. Country nightclubs are often incredible
places. On a crowded night, the atmosphere is electric,
with women on the prowl, stalking around in tight jeans
looking for action. The men are high on alcohol and
testosterone and looking for trouble of one kind or
another. Meanwhile, there are lighted beer signs, pool
tables, smoke, beer, video poker, and pinball machines.
The vibe is great. Music is blasting from the stage and
men and women have paired off, scooting around like
crabs across the sawdust-covered dance floor. Over in the
corner, an initial dance has led to an intimate conversation between a man and a woman, one which may be
concluded elsewhere before the end of the night, possibly
in the seat of a pickup truck out in the parking lot.

Many people feel that the nightclub is the real home of
country music. While this is certainly debatable, it is
probably safe to say that, over the years, clubs have
supported country music more than any other outlet,
with the possible exception of fairs and rodeos. Nevertheless, I do not know of any music business executives who
spend much time at country nightclubs. Managers and
agents occassionally put in an appearance, as do some
lower-level record people.

In fact, most artists do not like to play clubs. There are
many reasons for their reluctance. In the first place, the
club owner often expects two shows from the artist,
whereas the concert promoter requires only one. Also,

shows at clubs usually start and run late, with showtimes at ten P.M. and midnight or eleven P.M. and one A.M. being fairly standard. While the sound system in some clubs is very expensive, it almost never equals that of a theater, showroom, or auditorium. In addition, clubs are almost always filled with smoke, since tobacco and alcohol seem to go hand in hand. Add to this a number of drunk and rowdy patrons, and it's easy to see why many artists would rather play concerts.

The Supper Club

The supper club is a nightclub of a different sort. It usually has two shows per night, with either two dinner shows, or a dinner show and cocktail show. The admission price includes dinner followed by a performance by the headliner. Often, there will be a comedian opening the show and warming up the audience. These clubs are preferable to honky-tonks for the average artist because he is less likely to find a bunch of drunks shouting and raising hell. The sound is usually better, the audience more attentive, and the overall atmosphere more intimate. Reservations are usually required and credit card orders are taken over the phone.

Casino

Casino entertainment is usually divided into three sections. The first may consist of a guy with a guitar and a drum machine playing happy hour at a bar on one end of the casino floor. Seating is limited to a bar and a few tables.

The casino lounge is the next step up and offers gamblers an opportunity to chat and have a few drinks and in many cases a meal before resuming play. The entertainment is always more serious than in the cocktail lounge or bar, and most of the entertainers are professional and are generally accompanied by a band. There are specific show times, and patrons often come to see a particular artist. Seating in the casino lounge is usually less than three-hundred, but not always.

The casino's main showroom is set up much like the supper club and usually offers two shows, one of which may be a dinner show. The primary difference in this case is that the entertainer is used as a magnet to draw people into the casino, so that they will spend money gambling before and after the show. The entrance to the showroom is always off the main casino floor, so that there is a good chance of snagging patrons on the way in. Inside the showroom, there is table and booth seating, and you may end up sitting at a table with someone you don't know. There is usually a drink minimum, and the drinks are notoriously small. The sound system is usually very good, and most seats provide a good view of the stage.

In the casino setting, everything is expected to be extravagant, and usually is. The show in the main room is usually opened by a comedian, dancers, or some other type of performance not likely to be generally available in hometown America. Show length for the headliner usually runs about fifty minutes, before the audience is disgorged onto the main casino floor, hopefully to stay awhile and spend some money.

These shows are excellent for entertainers. No travel is involved, rooms are usually provided by the casino, and food is usually free for the artist and either free or discounted for the artist's band members and crew.

There is no room for artist grandstanding and lengthy encores in this environment, or for the artist with a bad attitude. Artists who perform beyond the casino's time limit on stage won't be around long on the casino circuit.

It should be mentioned that all casino entertainment directors know the competition. They know which acts are going to be where, and when. They also know which acts did well and which did not.

Some casinos offer the artist a percentage, or "four-wall" deal, in which the casino or house takes a certain part of the income from the door and the artist gets the rest. This arrangement usually applies to the artist on the way up or on the way down. It should also be mentioned that there are pitfalls for the artist inherent in the very nature of this kind of deal. If the place doesn't advertise properly, or if there are several really famous acts in town at the time, it's likely that the artist on the percentage deal with no guarantee will suffer financially as a result.

Percentage Deals

A percentage deal means that the artist will be making some or all of his income based upon a percentage of the money that comes through the door. This is known as a "door deal," and is the same thing as a four-wall deal. Why would an artist take a percentage date? It would seem that he would rather be paid what he normally receives and go on about his business. Let's say that an artist usually gets $25,000 a night. Perhaps he needs a pick-up date and there is no place en route which will pay him his fee. He might take a chance on a lower guarantee against a percentage, or he may have to take a straight percentage deal in order to work at all.

In the case of a large auditorium, a percentage date becomes a necessity. If the place has a $100,000 potential revenue gross, then the artist would not want to work it for a flat fee of only $25,000. The percentage in this case serves as insurance. The artist gets his normal fee, and extra if sales reach a certain number of tickets. The artist's agent will be approached with percentage deals throughout the artist's career, most of which should be avoided. While percentage dates are a way of life, for the agent, buyer, and artist, some work and some don't.

In a concert situation, the artist should be getting his normal fee guaranteed plus a percentage of the gate, gross, or door, after the breakpoint. The breakpoint is a variable figure determined by a number of factors, such as auditorium or hall expenses and the cost of advertising, sound and lights, tickets, opening act, security, insurance, and so on. In other words, the talent buyer's or concert promoter's total expenses are added together. Whatever this figure comes to is the total cost of doing the show, and it includes every conceivable legitimate expense for which the promoter has to pay. A percentage of this figure is taken as a proposed profit for the promoter and added back to the cost figure to get what is known as a breakpoint. It may sound complicated, but it isn't. Here is the formula:

Promoter's expenses + promoter's initial profit
= breakpoint

The artist and the agent decide what the promoter's profit should be realistically. I always felt the promoter should make at least 15 percent before a split. After all, he's taking all of the risks. The artist is getting his normal fee anyway, and everyone else from sound and lights to security is getting paid, all at no risk to themselves. Some artists feel this figure of 15 percent for a promoter is way too high, while the promoter feels it should be higher. It is a negotiable figure.

The breakpoint is the figure above which an artist begins to make additional money. After the breakpoint, the artist and the promoter split all additional money coming through the door. It is very seldom an even split.

The artist gets the majority, anywhere from 60 percent to 90 percent. This being the case, it is in the artist's best interests to set the breakpoint as low as possible, since he will have already received his guarantee anyway. The sooner the artist begins to make money on the percentage, the better off he will be.

It's just the opposite for the promoter. The longer he can delay a split, the better the deal for him. For this reason, promoters have been known on occassion to pad the expenses in order to make money on the front end, before they have to split with the artist. This is why all expenses must be approved by the agent in advance, before the deal is actually made.

The promoter, when submitting an offer, must provide fairly accurate cost estimates on every expense. He can't come back later with additional expenses which weren't agreed to by everyone at the outset. In fact, on the night of the show, when the box office is being settled and the money divided, the promoter will have to provide receipt copies for all of his expenses, or the breakpoint will be adjusted downward on the spot.

Now we come to the most important figure of all, the gross potential of the hall or auditorium. If the hall seats 10,000 people and the ticket price for this show is $18.00, then the GP for one show is $180,000.

$$\text{Ticket price} \times \text{hall capacity} = \text{gross potential}$$

The gross potential of the hall is a major factor in the promotion of every show, whether or not it's a percentage deal. If the hall isn't big enough to cover the promoter's expenses, then it certainly follows that there won't be any money remaining for his profits. But the gross potential is important for a number of other reasons, all of which are significant in putting a deal together involving the artist, agent, and promoter.

The agent often uses the size of the hall to appeal to the greed of the artist in persuading him to take the deal, so that the agency will receive a commission on that date, and so that the agent can move on to other matters. For example, if an artist is reluctant to take a date, thinking, as most artists do, that he should be getting more money, the agent can talk about the high gross potential of the show and dupe the artist into doing what he should have done in the first place. The artist in such cases tends to hear that high gross potential figure, and that is the one which sticks in his mind. Actually, the agent has done the artist a favor by getting him a reasonable guarantee in the first place.

The agent can also use the gross potential as a psycological tool or weapon against the buyer. The agent may reasonably suspect that his artist isn't going to fill the auditorium in question. He might actually know for a fact that the last promoter who did a show with this artist in that particular city lost money. While most promoters have done their homework, others emerge constantly who have not researched the marketplace. They simply assume that all they have to do is come up with some money and they can call themselves promoters.

Let's look at a typical scenario. The fact is that in this hypothetical case, the agent would be thrilled to get $20,000 for the act. He would settle for $15,000. The buyer, however, doesn't know this. Be that as it may, the buyer still wants to get the act as cheaply as possible. The agent finds out that the auditorium seats 10,000, so the first thing he does, if he wants to reel in the buyer is start by showing concern with the breakpoint. "Look, I can't see letting so-and-so work without a percentage. He hasn't played that market in two years, and he made a lot of money that last time. That has always been a great market for us. I don't think we can work for you in that city anyway, we had promised promoter Felix Hamster a shot at that area, but tell me what you've got in mind and I'll see what I can do."

The whole idea is to get that promoter thinking about that high gross potential figure and how much he is going to make in terms of his percentage. While he is busy negotiating points at the back end of the split, the agent will usually get the artist's regular and sometimes even highest fee by playing on the promoter's greed and gullibility, pretending to be more concerned about the breakpoint. In reality, the agent is glad that he got the artist's fee. To hell with the percentage, because he knows that the artist in question won't sell anywhere near that many tickets and will never even reach the breakpoint, let alone get into the percentage. In this case, the percentage is academic and only exists to lure the promoter into a false sense of security, not with the intention of defrauding the promoter, but with the desire to get the artist's fee.

So the final deal for everybody in a concert percentage situation will be something like this: The artist is to receive his fee plus a certain percentage over break.

There are often variations on the above formula, but it is almost always the cleanest. The easiest variation is for the buyer to guarantee the artist, say, $5,000 against 70 percent of the door, whichever is greater. In this case, the artist gets paid a minimum of $5,000 whether the place is packed or nobody shows up at all. In round figures, if the total gate receipts equaled $10,000, the artist would end up with $7,000, or 70 percent of the door, instead of his $5,000. The figures which I have chosen for these examples are purely arbitrary.

Another variation of the percentage situation is the structured bonus. In this instance, the artist is guaranteed a certain amount, win, lose, or draw. When ticket sales reach a certain point, then he gets an additional stated flat amount, say another $500 at 2,000 tickets sold. The bonus may remain at a fixed amount, or continue in increments of $500, or it might escalate to $1,000 at a certain point, and then to $750, and so on. Again, this is all negotiable.

While there are still other variations of the percentage deal, here is the last one of any consequence. In this case, there is no guarantee for the artist, other than that he receives the first $5,000 through the door, then the promoter gets the next $2,500, and then they split fifty-fifty anything after that. Again, the figures are arbitrary. I merely point out that in theory, many types of deals are possible. Most of those examined above are not in the artist's best interests.

Frequently a buyer or promoter will attempt to persuade the agent to work on a straight percentage in order to avoid having to pay the artist. Some of the arguments used by the promoter are flawless. "Hey, your artist wants $15,000. Let's run a $15 ticket. I will rent the auditorium, pay the opening act, and we can split the gate. If he sells only 2,000 seats, he'll still make his $15,000, and a hell of a lot more. The place seats 6,000, so there's a $90,000 GP. Your act could easily make $30,000, $45,000 if he sells out."

While the logic seems to be correct, many things could go wrong for the artist if a deal of this nature is accepted. In the first place, the promoter may not know what he's doing, regardless of his credentials. He might not have sufficiently researched the marketplace, in which case he might not know that some big box office draw is playing down the road thirty miles away the previous week. A big show a week early can take all of the money out of the area for the next month or longer. Also, in some places, many residents work in factories where they are only paid on the first and the fifteenth of the month. If a promoter tries to put on a concert a couple of days before payday, he may find that nobody shows up. Or the promoter, in an attempt to get something for nothing, may not advertise properly.

The best thing an agent can do is tell the buyer that the artist is not in the business of promoting dates and doesn't wish to be involved in any partnership with anybody he doesn't know. "Look," the agent says, "If we wanted to promote shows, we would rent a hall ourselves and take all the money." You can't blame the promoter for trying to get something for nothing, but, like I said, deals like the above are seldom in the artist's best interests.

The Multidate Promoter

While one can find European promoters, well-established domestic concert promoters, and fair producers who promote tours of country artists, the unestablished multi-date promoter is someone who poses a threat to even the seasoned agent. It is easy enough for a promoter to send a 10 percent deposit on a number of future dates.

As the dates get closer, the promoter starts rearranging the schedule, switching dates and cities. The other 40 percent of the deposit is due, most likely sixty days before the first shows. The promoter stalls further until it's almost thirty days prior to the run of dates and the money still hasn't been received by the agency. Soon it becomes evident that the promoter hasn't been able to come up with the rest of the money, and the artist is out of work for a two-week stretch, and the agency is on the verge of losing an act because somebody at the agency should never have let matters progress to this point.

Every agent wants to believe that the best possible scenario will happen, but usually knows better somewhere in the back of his mind. If an inexperienced promoter wants to promote multiple dates on an artist in some questionable markets, it's best to get 100 percent immediately. The agent can't afford to wait for deposits based on advance ticket sales.

The Festival Promoter

Usually about once a year, somebody gets the bright idea to put on a country version of Woodstock. It will be a big affair with major acts on all day and most of the night for three consecutive days. It will be in a big field with camping, souvenir booths, and so on. The agent who is tempted to involve his act in one of these fiascos had best get all of his money in advance.

While these dates sometimes work, the majority of the time they do not. Since the agent exists to do business, the best thing to do is to get half the money at the time of the contract, and then a month after that, while there is still money in the pot, the agent should call in the other half of the money as he is entitled to under the provision in his contract which allows him to do so. The money will most likely run out soon enough, but he will have secured all of the money for his artist in advance.

Other Promoters to Avoid

There are certain promoters every agent should avoid. That the agent deals with them anyway is the result of the constant pressure he is under to find dates for his artists. These marginal promoters are always trying to hustle some deal by the seat of their pants. The most dangerous use other people's money. They fall into several categories:

1. The sincere promoter. This guy really thinks that he can promote a winning show, but doesn't personally have the money to put one together. He will do his homework

to the best of his ability, find an investor, and may actually succeed in promoting a few marginally success- ful shows before he takes a big loss and is abandoned by his investor. He will move on to another investor, give references of the shows he's promoted, neglecting to mention however, the shows where his investors lost large sums of money.

2. The dishonest promoter who has some experience as a promoter but has never made any money for any investor. This guy is the most dangerous of all, because it doesn't really matter to him whether the show makes money or not. He's being paid by the investor (usually in advance), win, lose, or draw. When an agent who is under pressure to sell dates meets one of these guys ready to spend someone else's money, the artist is in danger.

In the past, if a buyer had sent in the signed contract and deposit, he could force the artist to show up, even though there was a strong likelihood that the artist wouldn't get the second half of his money.

Most agencies now have a provision on the back of the contract in small print which allows the agency to call for the balance of the artist's money in advance in the event that the agent feels that there is some chance that the artist might not be paid the rest of his money. This condition would exist if there were extremely low ticket sales a week before the show, or if the promoter had failed to pay another artist. The key here is the wording of the provision, which varies from agency to agency.

3. The most common of all bad promoters doesn't have enough money to do a show of any kind. He is easily recognized by his actions. His contracts are almost always late in getting signed and returned to the agency. Despite the fact that he is supposed to send a cashier's check for a deposit, this promoter is likely to send a company check.

This check may or may not bounce. In any case, the promoter has bought some time. By now the agent is sweating, and other agents at the agency, only too willing to see the worst, are telling the agent that the date is no good.

The third type of promoter is every agent's worst nightmare, and yet his greatest hope. He is neither honest nor dishonest. If things are going well, he's honest; if not, he'll say or do whatever is necessary to get by. Often he hopes to sell enough tickets in advance to pay the deposit to the agency. He comes through often enough so that agents take chances they shouldn't. The bad news is that his dates fall through often, and usually at the worst possible times. Anytime an agent sells a date to this type of promoter, there are many problems from beginning to end, and no rest until after the date has been played and paid.

Here's how it works. A would-be promoter finds some rich sucker and talks him into putting up the money to promote a show. The promoter may or may not actually handle the money himself. If the investor has any intelligence, he will handle the money, and write checks when necessary, and only after checking things out himself.

The promoter may structure payment for himself in a number of ways. Usually he will receive some money in advance to pay him for his services while he is putting the show together. He might receive a percentage of the profits, but since there aren't likely to be any, he usually gets the majority of his money before the show actually takes place. He agrees to a percentage on the other end, making the investor think that there are likely to be large profits on the day of the show. He's covered either way.

By showtime, advance ticket sales are minimal. It becomes obvious the show is going to be a bust. The artist wants to get out of the date, the agent is in trouble, and the investor is about to lose his money. From here it's all downhill. Here are the options:

1. The artist chooses to get out of the date because of poor advance ticket sales and the fear that he won't be paid the other half of his money which is due at the show. Even if he does get paid the other half of his money, he doesn't want to be embarrassed by a poor turnout. The promoter may agree to the cancellation if the artist refunds the 50 percent deposit. In this case, the promoter is out advertising, hall rent, and other expenses, but he still has the majority of his money, after ticket refunds. If everyone agrees to this, the artist has lost a paying date, blames his agent, and the agency loses its commission. Not a good scenario for anyone. The best solution for the artist is for the agency to persuade the buyer that he ought to cancel the date. If the agent can make the promoter want to cancel the date, then the artist gets out of the date and gets to keep the deposit.

2. The buyer says that he has invested a large amount of money, has complied with every part of the contract, and threatens to sue the artist and the agency. In this case, the artist has two choices. He either decides or refuses to work the date. In the first choice, he will have the agent make the promoter come up with the rest of the money. If the promoter can't do so, then the artist is free. Again, the artist has still lost a paying date. If the promoter does come up with the second half of the money, then the artist will be forced to do an embarrassing date with a low turnout, or be sued and most likely lose. For all of the reasons mentioned above, the agent should be very careful with whom he works. Again, this must be balanced against the constant pressure to find dates for a number of artists who are basically crying "Feed me! Feed me!"

Deposits

A deposit is basically a down payment on a date and is the same thing as earnest money in real estate. The buyer pays a deposit in order to secure a date on a particular artist. While the deposit is usually 50 percent, if the date is in the future, say eight months away, the agency may let the buyer pay an initial deposit of 10 percent with the contract, and another 40 percent closer to the time of the date. The deposit serves several purposes. It assures the buyer that he actually has the date. While signed contracts should be sufficient, this isn't always the case. That a buyer can show that he has signed contracts and that the agency accepted his deposit puts him in a much better position legally if the agency or the artist should get a higher offer and want to get out of the date.

The deposit also serves as a confirmation to the agent and to the artist that the contracted date really exists. A promoter who has paid a deposit of 50 percent has some money invested in the date which he isn't going to get back unless the artist cancels the date. The agent and the artist can both relax as soon as the deposit is in-house. The fact that the buyer has a financial stake in the date also increases the likelihood that the date will be properly promoted with adequate advertising.

Another, and perhaps the most important, reason for the deposit is that it separates the men from the boys, and the talkers from the walkers. Many people want to be promoters but aren't. They are, however, very capable of wasting the agent's and the artist's time and money. They lead the agent into a false sense of security by acting as if they know what they are doing. Contracts are sent to the buyer, weeks pass, and they don't come back.

If a buyer has a reputation for being shifty, it's not uncommon to require a 50 percent deposit before the

agent even sends contracts. That someone is able to pay a
50 percent deposit usually indicates that he can probably
afford to do the date.

While many agents knowingly accept dates from risky
buyers, ideally an agent would prefer to deal only with
someone who can afford to put on a series of shows, lose
money on all of them, and suffer no dent in his financial
well being. If a buyer sends in a deposit of 50 percent and
then cancels the date at the last minute, it's not as likely to
be considered the agent's fault if there is a deposit of 50
percent in hand. If a date fails to materialize, and the
agent did not get a deposit, he will be rightly blamed for
the problem, both by his associates and by the artist. The
deposit is the agent's insurance policy.

Nobody wants to pay a deposit, and many buyers and
promoters don't have to pay deposits at all. Most large
fairs and rodeos don't pay deposits. Military bases, as a
rule, don't offer deposits, and many colleges and casinos
will not pay deposits. In the case of the promoter who isn't
required to pay a deposit, not having to do so is the result
of having paid many deposits in the past and having
developed a reputation as a solid promoter, someone who
is good for the money personally whether the date is a
moneymaker or a bust.

There are legitimate reasons for not wanting to pay
deposits. If a promoter is a full-time talent buyer, having
deposits out to agencies all over the country for dates on a
number of different artists can tie up a great deal of
working capital. While all promoters want to get to the
point that they don't have to pay deposits, it's almost a
given that sooner or later the average promoter is going to
get in over his head. If an agent can make a point of
always getting a 50 percent deposit, he will be much
better off. Asking some people for a deposit offends them,
because it makes them feel as if you don't trust them. If

somebody acts offended, don't worry—they'll get over it if they want to do business.

Cancellations

The worst thing which can happen for any buyer, in most cases, is a cancellation. If the date is an annual event, a corporate meeting, a convention, or any other date which can't be moved, the scenario is worse still. Artists cancel dates for a number of reasons. While some acts cancel because they are drugged up or drunk, this is the exception these days. Usually a cancellation occurs due to sickness, a death in the family, or some other problem. Most contracts still stipulate that an artist may cancel a date if a movie part or a casino date becomes available. Some buyers cross out any cancellation clauses prior to signing the contract.

When a cancellation does happen and can't be avoided, the best thing the artist can do is to have his agent offer the buyer a makeup date at a reduced price and then assist the promoter in finding an appropriate replacement as soon as possible. The deposit should be returned to the buyer immediately.

It is not uncommon for a promoter to continue to advertise a multiact show even after having been informed by the agency that one of the acts won't be able to be there. This is especially true if the act cancels with less than a week to go. The promoter then continues to advertise the canceled act anyway. He can justify this by saying that it's too late to change his advertising or tickets, which it may be.

Usually the promoter continues to advertise the act because he gets the ticket value of the artist without having to actually pay him. If, on the actual night of the show, some people want their money back, he may have to refund some tickets, but chances are that the people who have already gone to the trouble to get to the show will stay there.

The cancellation is always a problem for the agency, since it loses the commission it would have made if the date had played. The agency must placate the buyer as best he can under the circumstances and at the same time keep his act from getting sued.

When the buyer cancels a date on short notice, the agent gives the deposit to the artist, minus his 10 percent commission. Sometimes, though not often, a cancellation by a buyer or promoter can be a blessing in disguise. If the agent can find another date for the artist, even at a lesser price, this cancellation in conjunction with the 50 percent deposit already in hand can bring the artist more money for the night than he would have had otherwise. Generally speaking, however, when a buyer cancels a date, it usually becomes a problem for the agent, who has to go out and find a replacement date.

The Declining Club Market

There are not as many active talent-buying clubs as existed ten or twenty years ago. In the past, a top agent could almost support a new recording act in the state of Texas alone, if the act was any good and was getting, or even likely to receive, radio airplay. People were curious to see the new act and to see if he was likely to make it. Clubs played a very important part in the process of launching any new country act. This is still true today. The difference between now and twenty years ago is that a new act could be booked for $2,000 or $2,500 and did not necessarily have to be subsidized by the record label.

The importance of clubs was a continuing factor in an

artist's career. Clubs were often the only buyers for a new act in the early stages of his career. They couldn't always afford the act after he reached a certain level, and the act would forsake the club, move on, and play auditorium shows to a much larger audience and for more money.

Even when an artist earned big money at auditorium shows in major cities, it was still possible to pick up an off night at a club en route to a concert in a larger city. Then, on the way down, when auditorium promoters no longer wanted the act, he could return to clubs and still make a good living. Some clubs, such as Billy Bob's and the late Gilley's, could pay as much as $50,000 a night for an act and were an ongoing integral source of income throughout an artist's career.

The situation has changed considerably for many reasons. In the first place, the club atmosphere is not as open to expensive live entertainment as it once was. In the Jimmy Carter era, when the economy was a disaster and interest rates were astronomical, the working man couldn't afford a new car or house, but he could afford to party on weekends. He might have worked all week, but by God, Merle Haggard was coming to town and he was going to take the little lady out on the town for a big night. They could return to their financial problems on Monday.

Now, and for some time, interest rates have been low enough that people who formerly went to clubs, raised hell, and got drunk can afford a house or a new car. Many of these people are now staying home and raising families. The prices for home electronics items have plummeted, and VCRs, which were once luxuries, can be bought by anybody for $150.

Since clubs have long been the backbone of the country music road business, country acts have suffered as a result. The bad news for the industry is that this shrinking club market is happening at a time when more and more acts are being dumped into an already flooded marketplace.

Be that as it may, clubs still serve as training grounds for the unsigned country artist. At a club, he discovers what it means to play three, four, or five shows a night. He learns how to work an audience, how to get its attention and win its approval. The club audience is a tough bunch, and they frequently express their displeasure with acts they don't like in unmistakable ways. For an artist with a record deal who isn't yet ready for the road, having a club as a home base can provide an excellent opportunty to make money and gain experience. Many famous and successful country artists, such as the former band Exile, Billy Ray Cyrus, and Alabama, have emerged to stardom after spending time and developing their acts in clubs.

The Club Buyer

Dealing with the club buyer can be a very interesting experience. They come in all shapes and sizes, from all walks of life, and in all personality types. I have literally had to wait to speak to club owners who had to be fetched from their tractors to get to the phone. Others can be reached only at certain hours on particular days, and if you forget to call them, you may have to wait until next week.

Timing is everything in dealing with the club buyer, so catching one in the right mood and at the right time has a great deal to do with whether he will buy something from the agent. Most of them stay up very late and are often in a bad mood when they finally do get to work. There may have been a fight the night before, some employee may be stealing from the cash register, or there may have been a malfunction with a refrigerator or the heating and air-conditioning system.

Having caught the club owner at an appropriate time, the agent must make his presentation. The object and purpose of the call is to sell the buyer an act, not to waste his time and yours telling him about an act. The object is to get him to buy something. At the same time, however, getting him to buy something quickly may be the result of months or years of developing a personal relationship with him, a lengthy, expensive, and time-consuming process.

Many club owners are cold, curt, and difficult to deal with, period. Others are that way until they have spoken with you enough times to feel they can at least associate your name with a particular voice. Some, perhaps the majority of them, are great after they get to know you, and will always show you a good time if you visit them.

In every case, the agent should know the person he's talking to. If it is a first-time cold call, the agent will need to get the buyer talking if he wants to do business. When an agent can get a buyer talking about himself, then the possibility exists of having a real dialogue, and the likelihood of a sale increases. Many buyers, especially at the local level, feel that the agent doesn't care at all about them personally and that as far as the agent is concerned, the buyer exists to be used. By engaging the club owner or buyer in a casual conversation, the agent can find out many things which will both set a relaxed tone and help him in his sales pitch.

Finding out a club's seating capacity enables the agent to quickly attach a dollar figure to that number and estimate the club's gross potential, a figure which will help him to decide which acts to offer the buyer. If a place seats 1,000 and the average ticket price is $15, then the club can conceivably afford $15,000 for entertainment.

"Turning the house" means doing a show, running everybody out after the first show, and bringing in a different crowd for a second show. While this is seldom done in a club as a rule, club owners are in many cases willing to consider it as an option if they want a particular act and can't afford the act otherwise.

While most clubs are likely to want a Friday or Saturday night appearance, many have a full house on a weekend night and therefore don't have to hire a nationally known entertainer in order to draw a crowd. The club buyer in this category is likely to use a name act on a weeknight, if at all. While weeknights are always considered tie-in dates in relation to a weekend, many successful five- or six-day runs for an artist start with a weeknight as the first date. The accomplished agent is happy to get a weeknight, since he knows he will be able to find a Friday or Saturday somewhere anyway.

While there are many similarities in dealing with any talent buyer, the club owner is generally using his own money, and for that reason, and many others, he may be the most difficult buyer to cultivate a long-term relationship with. Since very few country artists start out making $50,000 a night, the club buyer is the main source of income on the way up, and again on the way down, when the career is flaming downward out of control. For this reason, the artist will be wise to be pleasant to every buyer with whom he comes in contact on his way up the success ladder, even if the club is a toilet and the owner a thief and a jerk. All club owners talk to each other. Even if you never intend to play a particular place again, it's better to have somebody talking you up rather than talking you down.

One other thing should be mentioned about club owners regarding their importance in the overall scheme of country music. The club owner is almost always the first buyer to take a chance on any new artist. Usually the club owner uses a new artist repeatedly when he is getting started, often losing money in the process, while the artist is still basically unknown. By the time the artist has become famous, the agent sells him to a promoter for a concert date in the club owner's backyard, and the artist drops the club. The club owner, who has invested his own money developing the artist in the marketplace when no promoters were even remotely interested, is understandably resentful.

The best thing you can do, under the circumstances, is to call the club owner, thank him for his help in enabling you to reach this point in your career, explain the situation, and offer to work for him again at some unspecified time in the future. The club owner knows that this is the way the music business works, and that he will continue to develop new artists only to lose them when they reach a certain level of popularity.

Theaters

There is an explosion of theaters in places like Branson, Missouri, Myrtle Beach, South Carolina, and other markets nationwide. This renewal of interest applies not only to Las Vegas–type theaters at the new land-based and riverboat casinos, but to freestanding and hotel casinos as well. Entertainment brings people into these places, and the intention in many instances now is to concentrate on selling entertainment instead of alcohol.

The Military Buyer

The military buyer presents a unique set of circumstances for the agent trying to book his artists and for the artists who want to play there. Seemingly nobody has the authority to make a decision of any kind or to authorize or make an offer to buy an act. The person at the base will most likely have to get approval from someone higher up. The higher-up must get approval from somebody else higher still. Not only do these things take an inordinate amount of time, but the further one climbs the ladder of command, the less likely the agent will get the answer he wants. For these and other reasons, the possibility of an agent's securing a last-minute pick-up date at a military base for an artist passing through the area is nearly impossible.

Furthermore, relations which are established with specific persons within the military are often subject to abrupt change without notice. Military personnel are frequently likely to move about, go on leave, or retire. In these cases, the agent must start over again with someone else who doesn't have any authority, and explain everything all over again and send new publicity and schedules. The military buyer, under most circumstances, is more of a problem than a solution for the average major top-line agent.

The Fair Buyer

There are many different types of fairs, from the week-long fair or exposition which draws in excess of 100,000 people, to the small two-day fair known as a Punkin Roller, to the local one-day annual event such as a crawfish or onion festival. Just as there are different types of fairs, there are different entertainment needs as well. Most fairs want entertainment to serve the purpose of increasing revenue by drawing people to the fair. Others, usually the smaller fairs, merely want to provide the attendees with some good entertainment. In the case of the larger fairs, there may be a different major headline attraction each night.

The fair usually handles entertainment with either a free or a paid grandstand. In a free grandstand situation, the admission charged at the gate includes all live entertainment, including the headline attraction. When there is a paid grandstand, there is an additional charge, over and above the general admission price, to see the star attraction. Only a paid grandstand can provide an artist with a percentage of the ticket sales in addition to his regular fee.

Fair buyers are a unique group in that some of the major fairs have a board of directors who meet each year, plan the fair together, and jointly decide which entertainers to hire. In some cases, primary responsibility for securing the entertainment falls on one particular individual. This individual may be replaced every year or at other intervals, depending on the situation.

Sometimes the fair board knows exactly which entertainers they want for what night and negotiate directly with these entertainers' individual agencies. Often, however, the fair board is basically unfamiliar with the process of securing entertainment and may not feel competent to make the best choices. In this case, the fair board will meet, determine an entertainment budget, and then hire an outside agent or fair producer to supply the entertainment for the fair's entire run.

The Fair Producer

If a fair decides to hire an independent producer, then the fair producer will meet with members of the fair board, listen to their desires, and then make recommendations. If the fair board likes the suggestions he has made, it will authorize him to make the purchases he deems appropriate. The fair would like to make money, but in some cases, it really doesn't care one way or the other, as long as no money is lost.

Sometimes the fair producer is given the freedom to select whatever acts he wants, as long as they fall within the budget. At the same time, it is expected that the fair producer will get the best possible entertainment for the amount budgeted. Often the fair producer does more than just purchase entertainment. He may secure or provide sound, lights, and staging for the entire event.

Ideally, the fair producer will secure as many different fairs as he can for representation. The more accounts, the greater his buying power and the greater his income. If the fair producer can secure a number of different fairs, he is able to go to a talent agency and get a multiple-date discount price on certain artists, by offering the agency multiple dates in exchange for a lower price on the artists he desires. This is a good thing for all concerned. The agent is able to dispose of a large number of dates at one time, and the artist is guaranteed a certain number of dates at a time which is generally dead for indoor concerts in much of the nation.

While most artists are happy to get these dates in such volume, there are others who angrily refer to this practice as "double-dipping." In other words, the fair buyer is making money off the act, and so is the agency. Never mind that the artist wouldn't have gotten so many dates without a price discount to the fair buyer. The fair buyer or producer is after the best deal possible. If one artist won't do it, another will.

Deals of this sort are made in quantity, on different levels between the fair producer, the fair, and the agency at the same time. In other words, when a fair producer meets with an agency, he may be there to buy a string of dates on a $50,000-a-night artist for his bigger fairs, another series of dates for all of his midsize fairs, and several other acts in quantity for a string of local fairs.

It works like this: The agent sends a contract to the fair producer for Johnny O. for $4,500. Johnny O. usually makes $6,000 a night, but since the fair producer has agreed to take a minimum of twenty-five dates between the months of July and October, the artist has agreed to work for this individual at a lesser price. Any other buyer will have to pay the usual price of $6,000. In the meantime, the fair producer sends his own contract to the fair board for Johnny O. for $6,000. The fair board returns the signed contract to the producer, who then signs and returns the contract the agency originally sent him for $4,500.

When the day of the show arrives, the producer is there, picks up the $6,000 from the fair board, pays the act, and keeps the change. The fair board has received the date at the normal price, and is happy with the show and the fact that they didn't have to worry about any details. If things are handled properly, the act never sees anything but the $4,500 contract.

The act may complain, but the bottom line is that he got dates he wouldn't have received otherwise. The act figures that he is losing 10 percent to the fair producer in addition to 10 percent to his agency, and feels that if the agency were doing its job properly, the act would have received its normal $ 6,000 fee. If the act finds out that the producer has added $1,500 instead of 10 percent, he will be very upset indeed. The artist's logic is that out of a $6,000 date, he has ended up with $4,050 after paying his agency its 10 percent.

While the fair producer should probably be held to 10 percent profit, there are no rules which force him to do so, and perhaps that's not a good idea anyway. In fact, I've known of situations where a producer has added as much as $10,000 to an artist's price. The potential for add-on becomes greater as the price of the act increases. All in all, the fair producer serves an important purpose and represents an important part of an artist's overall income.

The Corporate Buyer

There are many large corporations which have national meetings, conventions, parties, or other get-togethers. Most of the time, an artist is hired as a result of someone contacting the agency in hopes of securing the services of a particular performer. The agent may succeed in selling the caller one or more acts. There are also smaller regional agencies which cultivate corporate accounts and serve as intermediaries in much the same manner as the fair producer serves the fair. The average top-line agency does not have the manpower to devote to cultivating this lucrative but specialized market on a full-time basis, and so most bookings are the result of call-ins.

Self-Promotion

Many artists, when they reach a certain status, decide to attempt some shows on their own. In this case, the artist either hires someone in-house to promote the dates or hires an outside promoter on a per-date basis and pays him somewhere in the neighborhood of 10 percent plus some points as a bonus situation if the show reaches a certain level of ticket sales. In either case, the artist picks up all of the expenses associated with the show, including security, hall rent, opening act, tickets and box office, sound and lights, stagehands, advertising, and so on.

This can be a very good situation for a popular artist, because he gets all of the money, instead of having to share it with some promoter. The downside is for the local or regional promoter who has used the artist for years and then suddenly not only loses that opportunity but has the act competing with him in his own backyard. In most cases, when an artist decides to be involved in self-promotions, he doesn't pay commissions to the agency on these dates.

The College Buyer

The college buyer is like the military buyer in a number of ways. In the first place, the person the agent needs to speak with may be difficult to reach. In most cases, this is a student who must be called at specific times, since he is likely to be in class most of the day. Like the military buyer, the student buyer must usually get approval from one or more other persons before a deal can be made. Also, as with the military buyer, the student talent buyer is likely to be replaced often by someone new, in the case of the student buyer, each quarter or semester. For this reason, it is difficult for the full-time agent to develop a lasting relationship with the student buyer.

Another problem the agent faces is that there isn't much middle ground for the artist wanting to play colleges. It's either the low-budget coffeehouse venue or the 10,000-seat auditorium. In the former, there's hardly enough money to justify the trouble, and in the latter, chances are that the college will be renting the auditorium to an outside promoter instead of doing the show itself.

While there is an annual homecoming show at most colleges and universities, it is likely that the student government association will meet and select a half dozen artists they would like to get. Consequently, most college dates involving any real money result from call-ins to an agency inquiring about the price and availibility of specific artists.

On the lower end of the scale, there is an organization called NACA, National Association of Campus Activities, which has regional meetings where a number of acts are showcased in front of college buyers. The act must be approved by NACA, must agree to certain conditions, and must pay a fee as well as all associated expenses such as the artist's travel and accommodations. In theory, this is a good thing because the act will be exposed to a large number of buyers who are in a position to offer dates at that time. For the average country artist with a bus and a band, this is hardly worth the trouble. In addition, any member of NACA is flooded with tons of unwanted literature.

The International Buyer

As the popularity of country music has increased, more international buyers have emerged who are actively promoting dates for a wide variety of country artists in different parts of the world. The Country Music Association monthly publishes an International Touring File, showing which artists are playing which cities and countries. This list also provides the names of the promoters and the agencies who set the dates.

The Telephone Promoter

The telephone promoter is a vital though often unmentioned member of the country music business. The telephone promoter approaches a charity, offers to promote a date under its auspices, and promises to give the charity a certain percent of the proceeds. In some cases, the promoter is able to get the charity to put up some of the money, but generally the promoter is content to use the name and services of the organization.

Becoming a Promoter

If it is your desire to become a promoter, you should start early. The best way is to get a job working with or for someone who is already successfully promoting dates for a living. You can check your local paper and see what company brings in big auditorium shows. If the print or radio ads don't name the promoter, then call the auditorium or venue and ask the auditorium manager the name of the promoter and where the company is based.

Having done that, chances are good that you will be able to reach someone from that company on the phone. Explain that you would like to meet with whomever you are talking to if that person will be at the show. If someone else will attend the show instead of the person you are talking to, get that person's name. Chances are that you can show up at the concert during setup, ask for the person in question, and say that you spoke with so-and-so at the office and that he said that "You would get me a backstage pass and let me hang around and see how things work."

Getting things done is a skill you need to develop if you want to become a promoter, or anything else. You can figure out how to get a backstage pass. One friend of mine walked in front of me through the backstage entrance at a show, flipped his billfold open and closed it in one instant, the way they do on police shows. He just kept walking and didn't slow down. I started laughing, so they stopped me and I had to explain a bunch of crap and finally wait until I saw someone I knew who would vouch for me.

The late talent agent Dick Blake said that if you need a backstage pass to get backstage, you don't belong there anyway. In other words, the power of your presence should be enough in most cases. He was right. Never wear a pass pinned on or visible, unless you will be going out into the actual auditorium and are planning to or hoping to meet some women. If someone wants to see your pass, make him ask for it. Practice not needing a backstage pass. This is easier to do, of course, if you have one in your pocket for backup.

A promoter needs to be familiar with every aspect of a show, including setup, sound check, box office settlement, merchandising, advertising, ticketing, catering, sound and lights, security, and so on. Working with any of these groups for a short while will give you a general understanding of how they work in real life. If you are in high school, get a job at the auditorium as an usher or ticket taker. This gives you a chance to observe many things in a short period of time.

If you want to be a promoter, you will need some money. Here, as everywhere else in the music business, money is just the start. There are many acts and agents who are only too eager to relieve an inexperienced promoter of his money. You must study the market you desire to promote. See who the competitors are, which promoters have already established a presence in the market area.

And find the stations you should advertise, see which have the biggest share of the listening audience you wish to target. See what kind of deal you can make with the radio station. Perhaps you can persuade the number two station in the market to give you a cut rate in exchange for letting it profess to be sponsoring the show. See what other events are scheduled, not only at the place you wish to promote a show but at competing venues. Be certain that the auditorium or venue you choose is in the right part of town for the audience you want to draw.

There are many things the promoter must be aware of and prepared for if he wants to succeed. Promoting dates is not an undertaking to be taken lightly. If you want to become a promoter, you must thoroughly research and study both the markets you are intending to promote and the artists you intend to use. Don't go in undercapitalized, and be prepared for anything from an artist canceling a date without notice, to an earthquake, tornado, or other act of God, or any other problem you could possibly imagine.

12

The Agent

The agent is one of the most important players in any artist's career. He finds the artist employment, places to perform for which the artist receives money. An agent of one type or another will be with every artist from the beginning to the end of his career. Agencies exist on different levels, and for the purposes of this book are divided into categories of local, regional, specialized, and major, based upon size, geographical scope, and significance of clients.

In most cases, an artist's initial introduction to a talent agent of any kind will occur at a local level. It is these smaller, local agencies that are handling weddings, college dances, shopping center openings, and other events. They may also serve as the exclusive buyers for some local hotels and clubs. It is on this level that an artist usually has his first experiences with an agency and agents. The local agency will probably book one-night gigs. Many of these shows will not be repeated. Other engagements, like those at hotel bars and lounges, may continue for days, weeks, or even months.

The successful local agency will constantly attempt, like its larger counterparts, to expand its territory and contacts. A local agency which exclusively books several lounges in nearby cities should ideally be able to alternate bands or other acts between the different rooms it books. In other words, a particular band can play in one city for three months, then travel to a similar engagement in another nearby city for another few weeks or months, and then move to still another city. In the meantime, another band follows one step behind in the rotation.

This is an ideal situation for everybody involved, including the buyer who is able to build up a steady clientele and minimize his advertising costs. Some agents have reported that while multiple-week engagements are still the ideal from an agent's standpoint, the trend is shifting toward the use of a different band each week.

If you are just getting started as an act and are ready to perform, then you need to establish contact with one of these local agencies in your own area. You will find listings for them in the phone book under "Theatrical Agencies" or "Talent Agencies." If acts are playing any- where in your town, approach them and ask them who their agents are. Contact that person or company, set up a meeting, and take it from there.

Regional agencies are a step above local agencies and usually represent a broader spectrum of entertainment. They also handle booking exclusively for several smaller but significant clubs, rooms, or hotel lounges. The re- gional agency will also represent more expensive artists than those on a local level and have more rooms in more and larger cities than the local agency. They may even book some impressive Las Vegas lounges and secure talent on occasion for important national corporations.

The regional agent, like the local agent, is still pri- marily room or venue, rather than act or band, oriented. Most acts represented by the regional agency are not likely to progress to the next level. Chances are that either the artist's talent or level of commitment either isn't there or the expertise doesn't exist on the part of the agent to move an act up to the next level.

In most cases, it is counterproductive for a regional agent to advance an artist, even if he has the means. The chances are high that he will lose the act as soon as anything significant starts happening. It is to the regional agent's advantage, therefore, to keep his act playing cover music to the best of its ability, as long as possible.

The third level is the boutique, or specialized, agency. Agencies of this type represent a specific form of entertainment, such as country, black, comedy, big bands, or nostalgia acts, and may do so at a high level, nationally and even internationally. Specialized agencies can be very large and do a phenomenal amount of business, or they can be very small, having only one or two agents and three or four acts. They may represent well-known, successful, and expensive national acts. The size of the agency doesn't matter either in number of acts or agents.

The most well known and by far the largest of the agencies are the majors. These agencies are the giants of the business, such as the William Morris Agency, Creative Artists Agency, International Creative Management, and others. They handle the careers of the most popular, famous, and successful talent in all fields, from musical artists in all categories, to the most well known motion picture and television actors, to comedians and magicians. Their range is international, and their influence in the fields of art, theater, and music is vast. The value of an association with one of these giants to an artist can be considerable.

However, unless he is a popular and high-grossing act, he will not be viewed as a priority act. The average country act on a major label will probably start with a local or regional agency and graduate to a major agency. If the act gets big enough, he may move to a smaller agency or he may remain at a major. Often an act will start its own in-house agency, stay there until its popularity begins its inevitable decline, and then return to a major agency once again.

How It Works

Dates are secured for the artist in a number of ways. Usually an agent calls upon an account and attempts to persuade the buyer to purchase the services of a particular entertainer. Sometimes an agency receives a call from a buyer who wants to buy a particular act or acts. This is known as a call-in and is the best thing that can happen to any agent. If a deal is reached between the buyer and the agent, they agree on a price for a specific date on a particular artist. The agent calls the artist or the artist's manager and gets the date approved. The agent then gives the information to the contract department, which prepares the contract and notifies the other agents that the date has been set.

The contract is sent to the buyer, who signs and returns all copies of the contract with the required deposit. When the contract returns to the agent's office, the agent looks over the contract once again, to make certain that no unauthorized changes have been made by the buyer. If everything is in order, the agent signs the contract on the artist's behalf or sends it to the artist or artist's manager for a signature.

While it is more convenient for the agent to sign all contracts, it is actually in his best interests if the artist or manager signs the contract. In this case, they cannot later complain to the agent that they didn't approve this term or clause. You may be certain that if any problem arises on a date and it comes to assigning blame, the manager will protect his own interests and blame the agent or agency.

After all copies of the contract have been signed, a copy of the fully executed contract is sent to the artist or his manager, and one is returned to the buyer. In many cases, a copy of the contract is also sent to the artist's musician's union as a matter of record. The deposit from the buyer is placed in an escrow account where it remains until the date is either played or canceled.

Most dates follow pretty much the sequence described above. There are of course exceptions and variations according to particular circumstances. Many casinos insist on sending their own contracts. The same applies to the military. Most fairs and rodeos don't pay deposits at all, and some colleges don't pay the artist until two weeks after a date has been played. While contractual arrangements may vary, the key point is that everyone involved in the process, from the buyer, to the agent, to the artist and his manager, has agreed upon the basics.

A couple of weeks or months prior to the date, the artist's road manager calls the promoter or talent buyer and checks in, making arrangements for arrival time, setup, and sound check. Eventually the artist arrives, the road manager picks up the balance of the money owed the artist, and the artist performs and proceeds to the next date.

When to Play a Date

Regardless of who's doing the booking, there are only a very few legitimate reasons for an artist to play a date. The first is for money, and the more an artist can make, the better. While an act is working primarily for money, long-term financial survival should be his ultimate goal. The agent must be able to get as much money as possible without putting the buyer out of business. Any great agent has probably killed several buyers financially in the early stages of his career. Being able to get an artist twice what he normally receives seems to be a wonderful thing, and there are times when it is appropriate, for example, when some zillionaire throws a private party for a few of his friends.

Some dates pay little or no money but are advantageous to an artist in terms of prestige. A classic example would be a White House engagement, or the singing of the national anthem at an important and well-attended, nationally televised sports event. Along with prestige dates are other dates which offer exposure for an artist. Dates of this type usually don't pay much money but are accepted anyway because they place the artist in front of a large or different audience which the artist would be unlikely to reach otherwise. An example would be an artist working an annual outdoor city festival in a large metropolitan area.

While an artist may work different types of dates, the bottom line for an artist on the road is how much money he brings home after all dates have been played and all expenses paid. "Routing" dates can contribute greatly to the artist's overall profit margin. A routing date is a date, usually an off night, on the way to or from a series of more important and higher-paying dates.

Routing dates are generally weeknights and are usually played for less money than other dates. An act normally earning $10,000 per night might be willing to accept a tie-in date for $9,000, for example, in conjunction with a date or dates at his regular price. He could schedule a Thursday date for $9,000, a Friday date for $10,000, and a Saturday for $10,000. He might be willing to work two more dates for as low as $6,000 or $7,000 a night. Routing dates cover agency commissions, band salaries, hotel rooms, and road expenses. They often make the difference, especially on long trips, between a financially successful group of dates and a losing run.

Dangers in taking tie-in dates exist for both the agent and the artist. For the agent, the danger lies in the fact that if an artist is willing to work tie-in dates for less money, the agent may be tempted to take the easy way out and not push as hard as he could or should for the regular money on other dates as well as routing dates. The danger for the artist is that if he is working for $10,000 and the word gets out that he has worked for less money in several other places, buyers will be reluctant to pay his normal or a higher fee because they think they can hold out and buy the artist cheaper. The agent can usually explain the situation satisfactorily to other buyers, but everybody must be on guard to see that the artist's price is kept at the highest reasonable level possible.

Often artists are forced to work shows which they would rather not work at all, due to political pressures. There was one banker in town who for years made loans to artists to buy buses, houses, boats, and anything else they wanted. The artists not only had to repay the loans with interest but had to do favors for the banker as well. These favors included playing free shows for charities or colleges which the banker supported. These concerts at the artists' expense increased the banker's social and political clout within Nashville circles.

Sometimes an act or band will take low-paying jobs at some out-of-the-way place in order to work on the development of their act, or to work in new band members, or to practice a new show prior to taking it on the road. Working under these circumstances provides the act the opportunity to be basically paid for rehearsing.

Commissions

Commissions may be defined as the money an artist pays to an agency for the work the agency performs. Commissions vary from agency to agency. Local and regional agencies tend to charge more than their national counterparts, and an agency fee of 15 to 20 percent is not unusual. Because an unknown act is not as likely to be in demand, most agencies do not fight over him at the local level. He needs work and the agency charges 15 to 20 percent. The act pays it and that's that.

While commissions vary from agency to agency, there is little fluctuation in the amount of commission an artist pays at the upper end of the scale. Just about every major act across the board, in all categories, pays a standard rate of 10 percent. While many agencies publicly state that they would never represent any act, ever, for less than 10 percent, the fact is that many will and do, when appropriate circumstances arise. If an act making, say, $10 million a year approaches a talent agency president and offers to move to his agency, but will only do so if the agency agrees to work for 5 percent, chances are that the agency will drop 5 percent like a hot brick in order to secure the artist as a client.

There are several reasons for this. In the first place, competition in Nashville among the talent agencies has reached phenomenal proportions. There are now so many agencies in country music that the pie of profitability has been sliced very thin. Any act which has a track record of generating high on-the-road income is a very desirable commodity for any agency. Whenever possible, successful artists use another factor which is to their advantage. It is the political and social clout that having them for clients brings. The popular artist provides prestige for the agency and also serves as a lure to other artists. Sometimes, as a result, highly successful acts succeed at negotiating a better-than-10 percent deal with their agency.

Split Commissions Versus Add-Ons

Situations frequently arise in which a commission is split between two agencies. An example would be where one agent is the exclusive talent buyer for a particular venue and another agent is the exclusive representative of a particular act. The act refuses to work for less than a certain amount, and the venue can't afford that much. In such a case, the agent might be willing to split the difference with the venue buyer in order to book the date for the act.

Another example is the buyer who has been authorized to book entertainment for a particular date. The buyer has been given a specific budget which does not include any money for his services. If he is to make any money for his efforts, he must be paid by the agency out of the agency's commission. In this case, when the date is booked and played, the act receives the same amount of money as he normally would and pays the same commission to the agency. The agency, in turn, issues the buyer a check for half the commission it receives.

Getting Paid by the Artist

The wise agency will not place itself at the mercy of the artist in the hope of getting paid. It's bad for the artist in that the agency ends up hating the artist and shifting its concentration to other acts. It's bad for the agency in that the agency usually keeps on booking the artist and is thankful to be paid whatever money it receives, regardless of what is actually owed.

The solution for the agency is to take commissions out of deposits in the escrow account after each date. That this is the agency's policy needs to be clearly established at the outset, when initial conversations with the artist are taking place.

Here is how it has to work for the agency. The agency will subtract its commissions out of deposits weekly, as soon as the date or dates are played.

If the artist plays a fair date or other date on which there is no deposit, the commission for that date will be withheld from deposits on other dates. It might sound confusing, but it is extremely simple. Any remaining money from deposits, over and above commissions, will be sent to the business manager, either weekly or monthly, along with an account statement. If the artist's business manager is a CPA, this procedure shouldn't tax him too much. In fact, it will actually save him time, since he won't be having to write checks to the agency.

The agency's survival is based on commissions, and there is no reason for an agency which has done its job to be in a financial bind because some artist is casual about paying his bills. If an agency has several big-money clients who are months late in paying commissions, the agency's livelihood can be seriously threatened.

The Two Questions

There are two basic questions every talent buyer asks when considering an act: "Do I want the act?" and "Can I afford the act?"

Let's examine the theory of booking. If an act is worth more than his asking price, he will work all the dates he wants to work. If the act is worth his asking price, he will work fewer dates, but he will appear many times. If an act is worth less than his asking price, he will work fewer dates, and in time, fewer still.

Many acts are priced not according to what they are really worth in the marketplace but according to what they think they are worth. "So-and-so is getting $20,000 a night. I'm much better than he is. Damn, my price ought to be $30,000 a night from now on." The agent receives a call from the manager, who informs the agency that the new price for the act is $30,000. The manager may know that this is an insane move, but he is afraid of the act, so he puffs himself up and delivers this ultimatum as if it were logical and intelligent. The agent, who knows better than anyone else what the act is really worth, also thinks the raise in price is a stupid move. He wants to keep the act though, so he gets the money wherever possible, leaving a trail of financial death and destruction in his wake.

When an act is overpriced, several things happen. Often the act prices himself out of a significant part of the marketplace. Buyers just can't afford to use him at his new price. As an artist's price escalates, the number of buyers diminishes proportionately.

There are a great many more buyers who can afford an act for $5,000 than can afford one for $50,000. So the act will lose some buyers who used him in the past but can't afford him anymore. The act will also lose dates that it would have gotten from people who intended to use him before the price increase but can't afford him now. He will also lose the possibility of any repeat dates he would have received as a result of playing these places. Also, the act which is overpriced is going to be working fewer and fewer dates in general. Consequently, he will be less visible and less likely to be considered as an option at all when buyers are thinking of their entertainment needs.

The agency, if it is any good at all, will be able to snooker a certain amount of buyers on an overpriced act. When this happens, and the buyer loses money, he remembers the agent who sold him the date and loses trust and confidence in his judgment. He may further wonder if the agent didn't knowingly sacrifice him just to sell a date. This suspicion causes the buyer to hesitate next time before buying an act from the agent who burned him. This hesitation or reluctance may keep the buyer from trying other acts he might have been willing to take a chance on prior to being burned.

So now one act's bad judgment or greed and the agent's fear are theoretically costing other acts money.

Behind the scenes, the buyer who has lost money makes a couple of calls and talks to other buyers, mentioning that he lost money on a certain act. He advises the other buyers to avoid the act, and they do.

In addition to losing money for one or more buyers and developing a reputation as a financial loser, the overpriced artist won't be playing repeat dates for the people he's hurt. By being overpriced, he will also miss other opportunities to play. The buyer with a specific budget will check out other acts in that price range and purchase the one he feels will offer the best overall value.

Since the majority of an artist's income is made by doing live shows, it behooves him to constantly monitor the dates he has just played. Did the buyer make money? Was he happy with the show and with the artist's crew? If the promoter loses money, the artist often automatically blames the promoter for not advertising. It's true that sometimes the promoter doesn't advertise sufficiently, but the problem most of the time is simply that the act didn't draw. The act was in town, and everybody knew it, they just didn't care or had other things to do.

After a while, if an act plays an area too often, nobody cares if they ever see him again. Since the money is good in such circumstances, the temptation for the artist and the agent to overplay a popular market is a strong one. Actually, an act shouldn't play a major market more than once a year, under most circumstances. Unadvertised private shows do not fall under this heading, since the public at large is not aware of their existence.

Selecting an Agency

The artist needs a talent agency if he is going to have places to play, and all agencies are not created equal. We have examined the four basic categories of agency and seen that an artist may pass through each type, as if graduating, and move on to the next level. The artist who as yet has no record deal and is unknown will be doing well to get whatever dates he can.

As he moves up the ladder, he will approach the great career divide which will put him on one side or the other of fame, namely the record deal. There are many acts who work local and regional shows, or even large private corporate functions and Las Vegas lounges, who do not have a record deal, have never had one, and never will have one. Some entertainers are very successful and make a good living financially, and yet they are at a lower level than any artist who has a record deal with a major record label. The local or regional agency may do well for an act without a record deal, but an artist with a record deal needs to be involved with an agency which is experienced in handling well-known national acts and acts on the way up.

The size of an agency is important to some degree, at least in theory. A large agency with several top-name acts offers a certain prestige to the artist who signs with such an agency. A large agency is also likely to receive more unsolicited call-ins than a smaller agency. In reality, however, the larger acts at such agencies will most likely get the most attention. Any agency's most important acts are the ones who bring in the most commissions.

It is felt by many artists and agents alike that the artist is best served by being at a smaller agency, where he is less likely to be shuffled around and where his needs are a real priority. This, of course, assumes that the agents at the smaller company are experienced and efficient. Actually, the best possible situation for any artist is to be the number one act at his agency, whether the agency is large or small. The prestige of being listed on a roster with other famous artists is a nice thing, but it doesn't put any dates on the books, nor do promises of TV and movies. Your manager and publicist can handle that end of things. That's what they're paid for. The agency is paid to provide income. If it can get some TV or movie deals, so much the better, but the primary job of the agency is to obtain dates for the artist.

An artist looking for an agency must be as objective as possible in making an important career decision of this magnitude. As mentioned earlier, just about any agent will say or do anything necessary to ensnare an unwary artist. He may even feign indifference, saying that he wouldn't take on an act he honestly couldn't help, that he has more acts than he can handle already, and that he doesn't have time to take on additional acts, no matter who they are. In fact, there are times in an agent's career when he will pass on an act for the reasons just mentioned.

Most of the time, however, it's to the agency's advantage to sign a new act with a record deal. If an act is going to make it, he is likely to do so within the first two or three years after his initial record deal with a major label. For this reason, it is in the agency's best interests to sign every new major label act it can get. If the act doesn't make it, then nothing has been lost, from the standpoint of the agency.

The agency will most likely want the artist to sign a contract. If you must sign one, the shorter the better. The most desirable and realistic period for the agency is three years; for the artist, one year. After you have signed a three-year contract with an agency, you have no recourse if it doesn't perform. Try to hold the line at one year with no options. A one-year contract with two one-year options on the agency's part is still a three-year contract.

The above observations generally apply to an act with a major record deal or an already established act with a history of chart success. The act which is unknown, has no record deal, and has no immediate prospects will be lucky to get any agent or agency. My advice is to do as much as you can yourself, booking your own act, and worry about an agent later.

The Responsible Agent

Within most talent agencies. there are certain divisions of labor and responsibilities. These divisions are generally established under the headings of jobs, artists, and geographical considerations. Anytime a new artist affiliates with a talent agency, he is generally assigned a responsible agent. The responsible agent is the one agent within the company who will handle the artist's day-to-day business affairs as they pertain to booking dates.

From the artist's standpoint, he does not need to allow himself to be used as a pawn in some power struggle between different factions at his agency. If there is an agent whom he likes or whom he has worked with before at the agency, he should most likely insist on having that agent appointed as his responsible agent. If this arrangement, or any other doesn't work out, for any reason, the artist should have no hesitation in choosing someone else at the agency to be his agent in charge.

The Territory System

Most agencies operate along a territory system. Depending on the number of agents at a particular agency, the country is usually divided as follows: One agent handles the Northeast, another the Southeast, another the Midwest, another the Southwest, and another the Northwest. In addition to these divisions, most agencies maintain a separate fair and rodeo department, and some agencies have a specific, separate department which pursues private and corporate-sponsored dates.

There are many advantages to operating an agency on a territory system, even though some agencies still use a primitive, backward, individual account system. The primary reason for the territory system is that it assigns specific areas of responsibility to agents. A top agency receives many call-ins, that is, unsolicited callers who want to buy artists for a specific date or dates.

In a perfect world, an agent would never have to make a single call but would merely answer the phone and take orders. In the real world, if an agent gets a call-in for a date in Idaho, Wyoming, or somewhere else far away, the agency must find other dates en route, to or from the main, or anchor, date. Under a territory system, the agent who accepts such a date on behalf of his artist is going to be the one who has to come up with additional supporting dates. He won't be able to rely on somebody else to cover for him. The same applies in each territory. If an agent plans to send an artist to California, or Maine, or Miami, he will have the responsibility of covering the date or dates in his jurisdiction with acceptable tie-ins.

Building a tour is of course much more difficult than taking a call-in date or booking a date somewhere at random. By having definite and clear-cut responsibilities, an agent develops his skills and learns how to set specific times to tour particular acts in his area. The agent who has toured an act extensively in his area also earns a much-needed break from the day-to-day toil of having to constantly find dates for a specific artist. He can say, "Look, it's somebody else's turn. This act has played too much in my area this year already." In turn, he can take some of the heat off another agent who has been working a different act at the same period in another part of the country.

There are still other reasons for the use of the territory system within an agency. One of the most significant is that the agent is able, over the course of several years, to develop relationships with the buyers in his area. He can learn when to take artists into his area and when to avoid playing there. For example, Friday night high school football is the kiss of death for shows in some places. In others, it's not that big a deal. Some areas of the country do great business in the summer, while others do almost nothing at all. The agent who has the opportunity to develop knowledge and experience in his area over time will also learn the needs of his buyers, and who is likely to take which acts and when.

Finally, there are other rewards both for the agency and for the agent. The agent who works diligently day-to-day developing his area will receive the occasional bonus of a call-in date. In addition, he will have the knowledge that he doesn't have to worry about another agent interfering in his area while he is out to lunch or temporarily unavailable. The agency will have the security of knowing there is no duplication of efforts. Furthermore, from a security standpoint, it is less of a risk to the agency to have an individual agent knowledgeable about only one part of the country rather than familiar with the entire operation nationwide.

Advice to the Artist in Dealing With the Agency

While many artists hold the opinion that the agent is no different than a used car salesman, con man, or carnival huckster, the fact remains that the agent, for most artists, represents the single most important key to the artist's financial well-being. Artists who fail to give this matter proper consideration are likely to find themselves in the rather unenviable position of being last hog at the trough.

As is common in every aspect of an artist's career, when the artist is at the top, he thinks that he will decide how things are going to be. Agencies are literally fighting over his representation. Every agency in the music business wants to represent him. The artist frequently makes the mistake of thinking that all the hubbub is about him personally. The artist considers himself to be a hot property and intends to use his fame as a bludgeon wherever possible against everyone he does business with. "If this agency doesn't pay me proper respect, then by God, I'll move somewhere else."

The fact of the matter is that agents are sharks. If they smell blood, they move in for the kill. While some members of the agency may like the artist personally or enjoy the artist's music, many won't and couldn't care less. The question for the agent is and must be, "Can I sell this artist for the maximum amount of money in the minimal amount of time?"

So here is some advice for the artist. As we've already observed, you fall into one of several categories. You are either an aspiring artist, on the way up, at the top, on the way down, or at the bottom. For most artists, life at the top is very tentative and short-lived. For this reason, you need to learn to deal with your agent in the proper fashion, which is to your advantage. As an artist, you are likely to have dealings with many different agents during your career. As you move up the ladder from local to regional agents and into the big leagues, you will be exposed to agents of all types.

By the time you are on a major record label and have been working the road for a couple of years, you should be locked into a good working relationship with a specific agent. Ideally, you should be your responsible agent's top priority. But how can this be accomplished at a large agency when the responsible agent you have been assigned to is in charge of several other artists?

The best answer to this question is another question. While you naturally feel that every show you give is the best you have ever done, the question remains: Are you going to be more excited working for $50,000 at a fair, or spending the same amount of time working a free show for some charitable organization out of political necessity? You are in business to make money. The prestige of representing a famous artist is nice for your agent, but it isn't putting any food on his table.

At Dick Blake International, one artist's manager came to the agent for the Southeast and offered to pay him ten percent under the table for every date he booked on his artist. The agent came to me and said, "Look, you handle Texas, Oklahoma, and the Western territory and are the responsible agent for so-and-so. I've been offered an extra 10 percent for every date booked on this artist by anybody at the agency. Why don't you put him opening for so-and-so and book him in your territory, and we can split that 10 percent?" The agency was still getting its ten percent anyway.

I thought about it overnight and accepted the proposal. As a result, the artist worked a hell of a lot more dates than he ever would have otherwise. We had an artist roster of about twenty artists at that time. If I had the choice of giving a date to one artist or another in the same price range, who do you think got the date?

Most artists are too cheap to understand that by sliding money to their agent from time to time, or taking him out to lunch, they can position themselves much better at their agency than other artists against whom they may be competing for dates. The relationship with the responsible agent should be cultivated throughout an artist's entire career. If you are a powerful and successful artist, you should let your agent use you as necessary to get a raise or strengthen his position at the place where he works. Of course, the details should be discussed in advance. Backing your agent in this fashion costs you nothing personally and ensures that you will remain his top priority. Whoever your responsible agent is, regardless of the agency, you need to be his number one concern every working day of his life.

If you as an artist are planning to move to another agency, discuss this in advance with your responsible agent. Tell him what your thoughts are regarding the matter and see how he reacts. If you have definitely decided to make a move, you should offer to take your agent with you to the new agency. Obviously, if you are a $5,000-a-night act, the new agency is not likely to hire someone you can't cover with your commissions. If, on the other hand, the new agency is eager to have you as a client, chances are good that you can force the agency to take your agent as part of the deal.

This gesture serves several purposes. In the first place, if you leave the agency and don't offer to take your agent with you, he is going to look bad. He was the agent. If he had done his job properly, so his colleagues will reason, you wouldn't be leaving. Offering to take him with you, even if he chooses not to leave, grants him some face-saving self-respect in the situation. He can honestly say that you wanted to take him with you but that he declined out of loyalty to the company.

Also, even if he chooses not to go with you, at least you asked him to. He may not like your decision, but he will appreciate your courtesy in offering and will be favorably inclined toward you in the future as a result. You never know when you'll be seeing him again.

I have represented one major artist on five separate occasions at four different companies over a twenty-year period. Let me put it like this: If you do make a move and your agent accompanies you, this puts you in the best possible position at the new agency. Instead of having nobody there who is intimately familiar with your day-to-day operation, and having to start from scratch, you will have your own agent already in place. He knows what types of dates you will and will not work. He knows what type of sound and lights you need, how much load-in time you require, and when you want sound check. Being able to make a smooth transition to another agency can save an artist thousands or hundreds of thousands of dollars. Your career can't afford six months of downtime while the agents at the new agency figure out how to book you.

More important still, when you move to another agency, the place you are moving to already has its favorites. Having your own man there ensures that you will be maintained as a high priority. Of course, the above assumes you have a responsible agent whom you like and are comfortable with. If not, the above will not apply. But remember, every time an artist changes agencies, there is likely to be downtime. On the other hand, the new agency may rush to set as many dates as possible in order to make a quick and favorable impression on the artist it has just acquired.

If you do decide to make some kind of under-the-table deal with your agent, keep your mouth shut about it. It's not something to brag about or to be ashamed of. It's a private matter between you and your agent.

The In-House Agency

The in-house, or artist-owned, agency seems to be a hillbilly phenomenon. The rock artist generally affiliates with one of the majors, pays his 10 percent, and is done with it. An in-house agency exists when an artist leaves the talent agency he has been with and starts his own agency, How you view this situation depends on which side of the fence you happen to be on.

In deciding whether to start its own agency, the act must consider several factors. There will be phone and postage costs, travel expenses for the agent, as well as his salary and that of a secretary. Does office space already exist, or will it become necessary to buy or lease property? These costs can be fairly easily calculated.

But what risks are involved careerwise? There is a certain safety in numbers, and being based at a large and poweful agency has its advantages. Furthermore, the agency most likely has a very strong fair and casino department. In all likelihood, dates in these important categories will be lost if the act leaves the agency.

Will saving $150,000 be worth the possible damage to the artist's career? Technically, the artist could lose that much by missing some fair dates in one season. While saving $150,000 might not be worth the potential risk to an artist's career, saving that amount or more over, say, a five-year period certainly is worth the risk. Any projections are based solely on the revenues of the particular artist in question.

The artist might even be able to lure some other artists to his agency by offering opening slots on auditorium shows. Potentially an artist-owned agency could begin by saving money but could build, and the artist could actually make money as well. Chances are that the artist who is thinking along these lines has already made a decision. He might not make the move today, but it is likely that someday he will.

What is the worst-case scenario? The worst thing that can happen is that the artist tries it for a few months or a year and it doesn't work out as well as expected. He can easily return to his former agency or move to another. It is worth the risk.

But what about the agency he's leaving? The artist's feelings on the subject are different than the agency's. The artist has paid the agency for every date it has booked. There has been no misrepresentation on the artist's part, and the agency is used to having artists come and go; it's the nature of the business. It has been a mutually beneficial relationship for the artist and the agency. The artist should leave on as good terms as possible, considering that he may be stealing one of the agency's top, if not its top, agent. All's fair in love, war, and business.

When an Act Leaves an Agency
(The Agent's Perspective)

Now let's look at how the agency should defend itself against the artist. The artist's contract with the agency has expired, or there never was one to begin with. All of a sudden, the president of the agency receives a call or a visit from the artist or his manager, or a chilly cease-and-desist letter from the attorney. In either case, the artist is gone. The agency is usually given two weeks in which to close any existing, outstanding, or incomplete deals involving the artist. It is not expected that the agency will be making any additional offers. In fact, the agency may be specifically instructed not to book any further dates in order to "give the new agency a fair chance." In some cases, the manager may give the agency only twenty-four hours to get together a list of pending dates, to ensure that no further dates are solicited by the agency.

What happens next is that the agency president calls the agents into his office, informs them of the artist's departure, and instructs them to drop everything they might be doing for the next couple of days and book every date possible on the artist, no matter how far in the future it might be. If the act is leaving, the agency might as well make every cent possible in the next two weeks, before the artist hits the road.

Everybody at the agency, including the act's responsible agent, may in fact despise the departing act, think his manager is an idiot, and detest his music. Nevertheless, if the act is a big-name moneymaker, nobody at the agency will want to suffer the loss in revenue or prestige which his departure will cause. For this reason, an effort should be made to keep the departing act.

The last thing anybody at the jilted agency gives a damn about is whether the new agency gets a fair shot at booking the act it is stealing. When the two-week grace period is up, the agents have a meeting to consider their options at this point. If the act is hard to book, they might just decide to let him go after all. Chances are, however, that the agents will assess their position and decide to ignore the manager and the new agency and keep right on booking the act as if nothing had happened.

In this case, here's what happens. The agents keep calling and pitching the departed act as if they still represent him. Many if not most of the buyers out in the field may not know that the act has actually left. The average buyer is bombarded by so many calls about artists anyway that it's hard for him to keep up with the constantly shifting artist-agent scene at all.

If an agent does encounter a talent buyer who has heard about the artist's move, he can simply deny it and say that it was an attempted but foiled plot on the part of the other agency trying to steal his act.

There are several possibilities here for the agency which has been left. If the agents keep turning in offers, chances are that the offers will be accepted, since few acts are in a hurry to turn down money, even if the act is gone for good. Another possibility is that the new agency will become hampered and exasperated in its efforts to book the act due to the continuing interference being made by the old agency and decide that the act is more trouble than he's worth. While this is unlikely, it starts the artist out on a bad foot with the new agency. If the old agency refuses to quit, it may just be able to retain the client.

The Life of the Agent

The day-to-day life of the agent is frought with danger from all sides. He often feels like James Bond, in the sense that five or six people may have tried to kill him businesswise before breakfast on any given day. The problem in Nashville is that in the past, there were only five or six agencies which more or less controlled the performance end of the country music business. Only one, the William Morris Agency, was an outsider.

This has all changed now. Other outsiders have smelled money and have flocked to Music City to feed off a form of music for which they felt nothing but contempt only a short while ago. The result for everybody in the agency business is that the pie has now been sliced so many times that there isn't enough, in most cases, to go around. As a result, agents and agencies must fight over acts which, under normal circumstances they wouldn't even bother with.

Few agencies can afford to pass on any major label act. Who knows whether or not the act will be the next Garth Brooks? So an agency must aggressively pursue new and upcoming acts, while at the same time seeking to steal big-name, high-income clients from competitors and trying to keep the acts it already has from being taken by another agency. In order to accomplish these objectives, the agency must expend a great deal of time, expense, and manpower.

While offensive and defensive strategies are an integral part of any agent's life, there is still the business at hand. The agency must set dates for its artists. These dates must be acceptable in number and price, or the artist will leave the agency and move to another. This is likely to happen anyway, even if the agency is doing the best job possible. There is always somebody from another agency telling the act or its manager that his agency can do a better job and can get the act more dates and more money. An agent will often make this statement with the full knowledge that it is a false statement. The lie repeated enough eventually passes for truth. Since most acts believe the last person they've spoken with anyway, such statements, if persisted in long enough, often succeed in moving an artist to another agency.

So we see that the agent is under constant pressure from many sources. If he books an act for Friday, then he needs to fill the Saturday slot also. If he books the Saturday, his work is by no means over. The act will want tie-in dates to accompany the two anchor dates. Technically, the act wants to work every day he is on the road. If one weekend is booked with dates to and from, there is always the following weekend to book, with tie-in dates. There is always two weeks from now, and three weeks, and next month, and the month after. It never ends, day after day, month after month, year after year.

In the meantime, the agent is constantly harassed, harangued, and threatened by the artist, his manager, and in some cases the road manager and band members. Multiply this by all of the artists on the roster and you get an idea of what the agent is up against every day.

It is difficult to imagine how many people assume that they are a better agent than the one the artist already has. Some dim-witted relative, lover, or spouse of the artist must be tolerated and humored. Everybody wants to be an agent and has some foolish opinion about how things ought to be run. Usually it is the person with the least experience, knowledge, or intelligence who has the most and loudest opinions.

In addition, the agent must constantly deal with the difficulties associated with actually booking dates. Dates are canceled by the buyer at the last moment without reason. A date booked months ago with signed contracts is suddenly in jeopardy because the last two acts were not paid in full or were given bad checks. Contracts come back from the buyer in an altered state or without deposits. The agent suddenly realizes that he has booked an artist at two dates fifty miles apart in a two-month period or that he neglected to mention sound and lights to the buyer.

Anything bad which can be imagined will occur sooner or later. I have had acts skip dates because they were drugged, or sick, or drunk, or the bus broke down, or because of the weather, including everything from blizzards to hurricanes. I had one artist cancel a date a week out because some psychic predicted that an earthquake would occur on the date of the show. For the agent, the possibilities for disaster are almost unlimited.

Nevertheless, and in spite of all of the pressures and dangers inherent in the job, any successful long-term agent will tell you that there are moments of incredible elation, when, for seemingly no reason, an agent enters into the tao of booking. Every date works out fine; tie-in dates in unlikely places seem to materialize out of nowhere. Artists are happy; contracts and deposits come in when they are supposed to. Every time the agent makes a call or receives an incoming call, it seems he is able to sell someone a date. The world is a beautiful place. Perhaps it is these incredible highs which make the rest of the job tolerable.

The Future of Agencies

As the country music business has expanded, it has become subject to the same mergers, buyouts, and take-overs which take place at the level of big business every-where. This is true of agencies as well. Almost twenty years ago, the William Morris Agency entered the country music field in Nashville by taking over the Bob Neal Agency, one of Nashville's original country music agen-cies. Since that time, the William Morris Agency has bought out the Jim Halsey Agency and either merged with or absorbed Triad, which had formerly been known as Regency. They and other large California and New York based agencies are here for the duration.

Others have disappeared over the last twenty-five years, including the Hubert Long Agency, Lavender Blake Agency, United Talent, Top Billing, Lucky Moeller, Dick Blake International, and In Concert International. For a season, each was the number one country agency in America. Others, like Shorty Lavender Talent, Celebrity International, the Nova Agency, Headline International, and Oswald Lobrecue Intergalactic, had their day and then passed into oblivion.

The future trend will no doubt continue along the same lines it has traversed in the last few years. The large agencies will devour the smaller but more efficient and successful agencies. But the talent agency business in Nashville has always been like a balloon. If you squeeze it in one place, it pops out somewhere else. So the larger dinosaurs can buy up every smaller operation on the map, but other ones will pop up in their place. Fortunately, many extremely talented individuals are still left in Nashville who cannot or will not work within a heavily restricted corporate environment. These agents will con-tinue to take important clients from the large agencies

and represent them. This constant undercurrent of movement, whether with agencies, in publishing, or at record
labels, keeps not only the music but the entire atmosphere
in Nashville vibrant and alive.

Jobs

The best thing for someone who wants to become an
agent in the country music business is to start as early
after graduating high school as possible. Again, the best
way to get a job as an agent is to find an agency whose
clients and reputation you admire. A listing of acts and
their agents may be obtained with a phone call to the
Country Music Association.

If you cold-call an agency, you are likely to be told that
the agency isn't hiring anyone right now. Here as
elsewhere, never waste time explaining who you are or
what you want to some receptionist or secretary. You need
to talk to someone who has the authority to hire you. Find
out who that is and learn everything you can about his
personal and business history as well as the clients his
company represents now. The best way to get this information is to ask. Even the receptionist will tell you who
the boss is and will likely give more specific information
if asked.

Perhaps the best way to meet talent agents is to attend
a meeting of the Nashville Association of Talent Directors.
This thirty-year-old organization meets at eight-thirty
A.M., the second Tuesday of every month, at the Nashville
Country Club. A call to the Billy Deaton Agency at
615-244-4259 will get the caller necessary information.

When you do talk to someone in charge, tell him that
you want a job. Explain to him why he should hire you.
Your objective is to get a job at any level within the agency
so that you may learn how things work. Don't be con-

cerned about how much money you will make. If you have no experience, you aren't worth anything. Be more concerned about getting the opportunity to learn the craft. Money will come later. If you are able to talk your way into a job in this manner, the chances are high that you've got what it takes to become an agent.

13

The Road Manager

The road or tour manager has several different jobs, depending on the size of an artist's overall troupe. A superstar artist will support a road manager, a travel agent, concession man, sound man, manager, tour accountant, security director, and several buses. Regardless of specific duties, the ultimate purpose of the road manager is to facilitate the artist's performance. If a road manager has done his job, the artist should be able to step on stage, perform, and return to the hotel or bus, knowing everything has been handled thoroughly and professionally.

In most cases, a typical tour scenario will proceed as follows. An agent books a date or series of dates. These are presented either to the artist or to his management, approved, and confirmed. The artist's manager or agent notifies the road manager that a series of dates has been accepted by the artist. The agent issues appropriate contracts covering each date, and contracts are signed by all parties. The manager or agent then provides the road manager copies of the contracts covering each date. These contracts not only indicate the amount of money the artist is to receive but also contain such information as show time or times, length of show, equipment load-in and load-out times, rehearsal time, if applicable, and sound check time.

In addition to the basic contract, there is a second, more lengthy part called the contract rider. While the actual contract covering an engagement is fairly uniform from artist to artist, such is not the case with the rider. This multi-page document is almost always unique for each artist and contains additional requirements which are necessary for the artist to perform the show. Generally speaking, these additional terms and conditions usually pertain to such basic things as stage setup, sound and lighting equipment and technicians, security, dressing rooms, bus parking, and so on.

With this information in hand, the road manager makes travel arrangements. If the artist travels by air, he contacts the travel agent, who checks the computer, seeking the best and most cost-efficient tickets available, making certain to either seek out or avoid certain airlines, according to the artist's preferences. He arranges ground transportation from the airport to the auditorium and back. If the artist is traveling on one or more buses, the tour manager checks the distances between cities, allows for travel time, and determines the most efficient routing. He makes hotel arrangements, seeking corporate or discount rates for the artist.

About three weeks prior to the first date, the road manager makes his first calls to the various parties at each city on the upcoming tour. The auditorium director and promoter are contacted in order to see that they have arranged to provide everything required on the rider. With the auditorium manager, in the case of a percentage date, it will be necessary to check the seating as to capacity, ticket price, dead seats (seats with obstructed visibility), and so on, whether it is reserved or general admission, concert or festival seating.

Concession sales are an important part of an artist's income. The auditorium charges the artist a certain percentage for the privilege of selling T-shirts, jerseys, cassettes, and other souvenirs. The rate fluctuates from no charge at all to as high as 40 percent. In some cases, the auditorium provides sellers and tables. In other cases, the artist must provide the sellers. The circumstances vary from hall to hall and from artist to artist. Regardless of the arrangements, the tour manager is usually the one who initially makes contact with the auditorium director and sees that everything agreed to by all parties concerning concession sales is in proper order.

After all arrangements for transportation, lodging, sound check, rehearsal, and show times for each date on the tour have been established, the tour manager prepares a tour book which contains every bit of information necessary for each date on the entire tour. This book describes tour activities on a day-by-day basis. It contains addresses and phone numbers of every hotel, auditorium, club, or other venue on the tour. The tour book provides flight numbers and arrival and departure times for planes, buses, and limos, to, from, and between every place on the tour. This book then goes to the manager, agent, PR firm, band members, the record company, crew members, security people, concession department—in short, everybody who has anything to do with the artist.

In most cases, the road manager is responsible for seeing that the money is collected at the show. Usually one or more advance payments have been made to the agency as contracts were executed by the buyer or promoter. In the case of fairs and some other types of shows, the artist is paid in full either prior to or after his performance. Collecting the artist's money is the tour director's responsibility. In most cases, this is a simple procedure. The road manager reads the contract, notes the amount of deposit which the agency has already received, and determines the amount still due. He accepts cash or a cashier's check for the balance of the artist's fee. While getting paid is usually a fairly simple and routine procedure, there is little room or toleration for error. The purpose is for the entertainer to get home with as much money as possible at the end of the tour.

Sometimes getting paid isn't that easy. In a frequently occurring scenario, the promoter will have sent in half of the deposit as required by the contract. He will have advertised properly but will have misjudged the artist's popularity, or failed to consider a competing event somewhere close on the same night. Whatever the reason, he will not have the other half of the money which is due to the artist at show time. He may have some of it or none of it.

What is the road manager supposed to do in this situation? There are several available options. First, the road manager will inform the artist of the problem. They will discuss the situation, blaspheme the agent, and then call the agent on the phone. Regardless of who should have done what, the artist is still faced with a very definite and immediate predicament. He has two choices: either do or not do the show.

If the artist refuses to perform because he hasn't been paid as agreed, he is likely to either anger or disappoint the fans who have come to see the show. In many cases, fans have gone to a great deal of trouble to get there in the first place. If the artist goes ahead with the show anyway, he is usually paid the remainder of his fee by a check, which is almost certain to bounce. Collecting on a bad check out of state is time-consuming and inefficient. It's a tough call. If the venue is a large one, with many empty seats, it looks bad for the artist even if he does play. Either way, the road manager will accept a check rather than nothing, but the agent will certainly have to answer to the artist when he returns home.

The road manager will often serve as tour accountant. This entails more than simply picking up the cash due at a performance on the day of show. He may frequently have to settle a theater or auditorium box office on the night of the show. Checking the attendance against ticket stubs and unsold tickets in this way can require a great deal of time, regardless of how well the promoter has documented his expenses.

The formula is pretty simple in theory, but not always in practice. The promoter has supplied an auditorium or stadium chart showing the number of seats in the building as well as their placement. The promoter or ticket agency provides a certified ticket manifest, stating how many tickets were printed at each ticket price. The figures provided by the promoter should match those from the ticket agency. In other words, the amount of tickets sold at a certain price should equal the amount of money received by the artist, minus agreed-upon promoter expenses. If there is a problem with the box office, it is usually settled before the show.

Keeping up with all of this requires attention to details and intuitive skills. The last thing an artist wants is to work a percentage deal of any kind and be cheated at the door. This can happen in a number of ways, but most frequently when somebody within the club owner's or promoter's camp lets a large number of friends or girlfriends in through the door at no charge.

For a road manager to be effective, he must have the confidence of the artist and the manager. The tour manager is less subject to outside attack than other members of the artist's camp, like the agent or manager. One reason is that everybody in the artist's camp knows that the road manager's job calls for a lot of hard work and involves a great deal of personal responsibility.

What happens if the bus breaks down on the road in

the middle of a tour? An important piece of equipment malfunctions? Some crew or band member can't be found when it's time to leave for the next city? There are literally dozens of things that can and do go wrong at any time. They may never be the road manager's fault, but they always become his responsibility.

Another common problem encountered by the road manager is the artist himself. While most artists understand the necessity of cooperating with the program, there are those who are drunk, drugged up, or insanely egocentric, or who just don't give a damn one way or the other. For whatever reasons, they refuse, and usually at the last moment, to do something which most likely they had already approved in advance. In such cases, the road manager must serve as press agent, psychiatrist, politician, advocate, friend, and jack-of-all-trades. He must instinctively know how far he can push the artist, agent, and manager without getting fired.

Maintaining order in such a detailed and potentially volatile environment requires great diplomatic skills.

Road managers are generally a decent bunch, but the potential for danger from the road manager always exists for the manager or agent. The road manager often spends more time with an artist than anybody else. In fact, if he is sharp, he will strengthen his own position by getting as close to the artist as possible. He will seek to become an adviser and close confidant. Due to their involvement with an artist, the manager and agent are the most susceptible to continual backstabbing from the road manager. But the road manager can also target a band member, the bus driver, or anyone else, for that matter, with or without just cause.

I have often been on the receiving end of such pillow talk and can state firsthand that the road manager can be a real inconvenience. The problem is generally first detected when an artist seems unusually distant upon returning from a series of road shows, especially if the shows have been financially successful. A chilly attitude at an unwarranted time frequently indicates that someone has been brainwashing the artist. While artists generally suffer serious mood swings, often without reason or notice, there are certain times when an artist picks fights or whines about things which are of no consequence.

In cases where the road manager creates antagonism, other players on the artist's team may drop their hostilities and band together long enough to get rid of a mutual enemy. If this decision has been made, then the road manager must be undermined quietly so as not to put the artist on the defensive. The artist must come to believe that it is in his best interests to dispose of the road manager. It is better still, if he thinks that it is his own idea.

Jobs

I asked several top road and tour managers how they were hired in the first place and to describe the necessary qualifications for the job. The older road managers, especially in the case of veteran country artists, tended to consider themselves to be babysitters. Most of them had started out as bus drivers or band or family members who doubled as road managers. They were not, as a rule, particularly concerned with details, and advanced the show, if at all, a couple of days out. They had done hundreds if not thousands of shows over the years and knew from experience that most events were successful. These road managers tended to have been with their respective artists for years and in all probability would retire when the artist did.

The younger acts seem to need as much production and as many buses as they can get on the road. In many instances, it simply means keeping up with or surpassing the Joneses. "So-and-so has three buses, I've got five." The same goes for road crews and production. It is a status symbol among entertainers to have as many people and as much equipment on the road as possible. An overabundance of unnecessary men and equipment almost always indicates a foolish and ego-centered artist. Nevertheless, the presence of all this equipment requires a road manager with a much less cavalier attitude about taking care of business than is required by an entertainer with one bus.

In the past, the road manager was likely to be some good ole boy, a relative or in-law of the artist, or some drinking buddy. On-the-job training is still the case now, but today the road manager or tour director is a different breed altogether. In the first place, he is likely to have some college education. He is also likely to be sharp, well dressed, and intelligent, realizing that when he steps off the bus at the show, he will be making his artist's first impression. That impression will often set the tone for the entire show. If some slob steps off the bus with beer cans falling out on the ground at his feet, it reflects badly on the artist.

What the artist seeks in a road manager is someone with skill, experience, and an ability to save money on the road. This means living within the budget which has been established by the artist's manager or accountant.

Since most artists derive the majority of their incomes from live performances, a skilled and experienced road manager or tour director is one of the most important people in the music business. The best way to get an entry-level job as a road manager is to first work with the road crew. This means the long and difficult task of loading and unloading stage equipment and gear and setting up and tearing down the stage and sound and lighting equipment. Working on the road crew would be the equivalent of a record company executive's starting out in the mailroom. The potential for advancement is there.

The future of the job of road manager or tour director, within the country music business, seems to be promising. With the increasing popularity of country music and with more artists touring, the opportunities are greater than ever before. For the person who can handle the rigors and responsibilities of this type of work, there is always room at the top if you belong there. At the very least, this job serves as an excellent stepping stone to higher things. The road manager for a successful big-time act will have gained valuable experience which will lend itself to important work in related fields, such as publicist, manager, agent, auditorium manager, concession manager, and so on.

My advice to anyone wishing to pursue this line of work is to find one of the best road managers in the business and talk him into hiring you. Be prepared to work for expenses if necessary. If you are sincere, it will show, and you might get an apprenticeship. Here, as elsewhere in the music business, those who serve as the top in their fields have earned the right to work for the biggest artists and to make the most money.

The job of road manager is usually dominated by males. While there are exceptions, males are more likely to be hired, due to their past experiences within the business, such as road crew or security work. Mainly, however, males are chosen because they are perceived to project a more commanding and, if necessary, intimidating physical presence.

14

Country Video

While radio airplay is still the most reliable and effective way to break a new country artist, the fact remains that the medium of video has opened opportunities that were unimaginable twenty years ago. It is now possible, through the existence of broadcast video, for the country fan to immediately associate a face and image with the song he hears on the radio. Perhaps the most important function of video in the artist's life is to create an identity. In fact, identity and recognition are possibly the single most important early goals of the country artist.

Before we examine the process by which a country music video comes into being, let's define some commonly used terms.

Producer: The video producer can be compared to a general. He is responsible for keeping the supply lines moving, ordering necessary equipment, working out transportation, feeding, scheduling, and so on. He follows the project from beginning to end, from preproduction through shooting, postproduction, and editing. It is his duty to see that when the director needs anyone or anything, that person or thing is where it is supposed to be, when it is supposed to be. The producer is also responsible for the budget, both for determining what the project will cost and for seeing that the money is spent in the most effective way.

Production Manager or Assistant: The production manager, or assistant, makes most of the phone calls, following the producer's instructions. He will directly delegate authority and see that details are implemented.

Director: The director is the creative boss of the video shoot, and will determine a shot list and set sequence for the filming. While he may work from a shot list, or schedule he has already prepared, he is likely to have a master plan inside his mind, allowing him to know which shots are essential and which might reasonably be dropped if time or financial limitations become a factor.

Assistant Director: Basically, the job of the assistant director is to yell at everybody, so that the director doesn't have to. Actually, his job is much more complex than that, but he mainly serves as an executive officer for the director and sees that the director's orders are carried out effectively.

Gaffer: The gaffer is in charge of lighting and works with the director of photography, translating his concepts into specific terms so that they can be implemented.

Grip: The grip is responsible for the movement and positioning of cameras and other equipment.

Art Director: The art director takes care of everything connected with the various sets and backgrounds. He must see that the sets are prepared for shooting and that they support the overall theme of the film.

Best Boy: The term "best boy" is another name for an

assistant or second in command. There is a best boy for each department.

In addition, a basic crew for a music video consists of the actors, sound technicians, caterers, security, cameramen, makeup coordinators, and wardrobe and prop masters. The creation of a successful music video is definitely a team effort, and each member of the team must carry his own weight. In the event that someone forgets to do something, there may be forty people sitting around with the meter running until the oversight has been corrected.

Editing

The editor is one of the most important persons involved in any music video and will fashion a finished project from the film he receives. He will cut, paste, discard, sequence, time-code, and generally rearrange the video into its final form.

In the editing room, the thirty-five-millimeter negative film is transferred to digital videotape. From there, it is edited and electronically reassembled. For an average three-minute video, a shoot of one hundred minutes of film is not uncommon.

Here is the process by which a video comes into existence for the signed artist, that is, the artist who has a record deal. The record company picks the artist's next single release, the record it intends to ship to radio. The audio version of the tape is then sent to a number of video directors, from as few as five to as many as twenty. The record company is likely to provide specific dates on which the artist will be available, a proposed budget, and a required completion date. On some occasions, the record company may offer the director specific information as to whether the video should be a performance video, a narrative video, or a concept video, that is, one with a filmed story line which more or less follows the song. Usually, if the artist is unknown, or if this is his first video, a performance video will be selected.

The director must submit a proposed concept for the project, such as location, theme, and so on. The record company considers each of the proposals, decides which one is best in terms of the way it represents and projects the artist's image, makes a selection, and contracts the work with the chosen company.

A preproduction time, in which preparations are made to begin shooting, may last anywhere from two days to two weeks. The shoots themselves tend to be one day shoots of fourteen to eighteen hours, partially due to the availibility of the artist. The cost of a music video runs generally between $40,000 and $80,000.

How could a one day video shoot possibly cost $80,000? In the first place, the video company will sub-contract a number of important functions to other companies who specialize in a particular field, like lighting or catering. There is no reason for a video company to keep a full-time caterer in house, on salary, and fully staffed and equipped. It's much more cost-effective to simply hire one as needed. The same generally applies to editing and camera equipment as well. Hiring these services on an hourly basis from outside specialists is very expensive. At the same time, some of the larger video companies in Nashville and elsewhere do own most or all of their own camera, lighting, and editing equipment.

It's not unusual for thirty to forty people to be on a set at any given time, all of whom are on the clock whether or not they are working at any particular moment. Often a country music video will have several different locations, sometimes in different parts of the country. Location and set changes of this magnitude require transportation costs for the crew, or the hiring of an entirely separate crew in the second or third location. In either case, there are many expenses involved.

A music video is essentially a work for hire, and the director or video company receives no royalties or any percentage of sales or pay for the number of times it is broadcast. Nonetheless, video production means big money to those who are given the jobs.

A company with an established track record is likely to be a strong contender for any job for hire. The term "established track record" means, in this situation, a company or director with a history of having done great music videos before for recording artists, in rock, country, or another type of music. Budgetary considerations also apply to some degree.

While the record company and the artist in theory want to keep the expenses as low as they can, the possibility exists that in fact, nobody really gives a damn. The artist in most cases is happy to get a video and wants the best one possible. The video will be charged against his account by the record company, and for that reason, lower expenses are desirable. On the other hand, unless he sells a lot of records, he isn't going to make any money from the record company anyway. That is, the record company will have to recoup its expenses before the artist earns any money beyond his original advance. If he does become a big star, he will be able to afford it.

How Does One Get Started in Video?

Going to film school certainly gives you a broad-based knowledge. There are classes on film history, cameras, and editing, and the opportunity to make films as part of class projects. At the same time, you are not likely to be asked, in Nashville at least, whether you went to film school. The point is to learn as much as possible by whatever means are available.

One friend of mine with a bachelor's degree in fine arts with a concentration in filmmaking started as a production assistant and worked his way up to production coordinator, production manager, line producer, to producer, over a course of several years. As a production assistant, he was receiving very little money. In fact, when he first started working after film school, he worked for nothing. During the course of the first year, he learned the job of production assistant and met enough people so that he was able to get a paying job, though still for not much money.

If you want to be a cameraman, for example, you could possibly begin by working as a gofer at a camera rental store or video production company. You will learn everything you might need to know about the cameras being used. Eventually your responsibilities will include the cleaning and maintenance of the equipment you hope to be using in the future. By the knowledge you gain working in this way, the possibility arises that you may get an opportunity to be hired as an assitant cameraman at some point, perhaps by one of your customers.

The Video Bio

We have discussed the "showcase" elsewhere, where an artist puts on a performance, hoping that record company people will show up, see him, and sign him to a record contract. It is increasingly more difficult to persuade top-level record company personnel, that is, those at a decision-making level, to come out after work to see an act play. In the first place, these people have listened to music, talked about music, and been involved with music all day. The last thing they want to do, especially if they are married, is to hang around and go see yet another artist for whom they do not have room at the record label.

A practical alternative is the video bio or press kit. This audiovisual presentation is likely to feature a music video, biographical information about the artist, and a short segment during which the artist tells a little about himself. From the viewer's perspective, a great deal of time, trouble, and inconvenience is saved, in that he can look at the video at home or at some other time that suits his schedule better.

The artist presents himself under the best possible circumstances, both musically and visually. The shots have all been considered, edited, and assembled to make the artist look and sound as good as possible. There is no room for error as there would be at a live performance. The artist will have no worries or fears about his appearance, sound and lighting, the band, whether anyone will show up, or any of the other concerns likely to have a negative effect on a live performance. The video captures and presents the aspiring artist at his best.

Much goes into the preparation and execution of a showcase. The hall or other place of performance must be rented, sound and lights must be manned and operated, the band must be rehearsed, calls made, and invitations sent. Even with all the bases covered, there is no guarantee that anybody important will show up to see the act, even if they said they would. Even those who have agreed to come are subject to emergencies or unplanned delays, with the result that another showcase may have to be put together, and all of the time, hassles, and expenses repeated, with possibly the same results again.

For these and other reasons, the video press kit offers an excellent means of presenting an artist at a reasonable price. The cost of this type of presentation varies with the individual nature of each project, but the cost for an excellent seven-minute presentation is less than $10,000 and more often in the $5,000 range.

Ultimately, the visual presentation of the country music artist via the music video is now and will continue to be one of the most important marketing tools available. For those interested in the field of video production or one of its many related jobs, there are now and will increasingly be opportunities available for lucrative and successful careers in these fields.

FINAL WORD

What Can I Do Today?

Ultimately, success in the music business is the result of a combined number of small successes extending over a period of time. The question for everyone, whether artist, writer, musician, or business executive, should be, "What can I do today to advance my career?"

This is a question which everyone should ask himself the very first thing every morning. The answer will determine the day's activities. Don't wait on someone else to decide your fate. You are responsible for taking the initiatives which will make you successful. See whom you can call, what appointments you can make, what you can learn, and what you can reasonably expect to accomplish each day. Set specific goals and approximate deadlines for reaching those goals, and then get busy. Your success or failure is ultimately up to you. Develop a flexible game plan and work on it daily.

Index